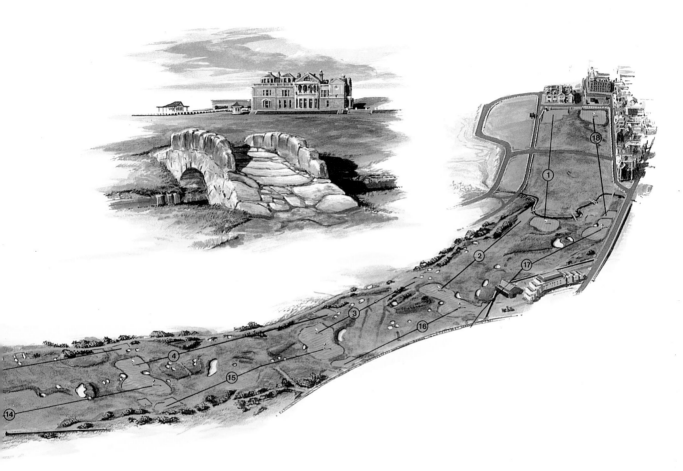

139TH OPEN CHAMPIONSHIP
Card of the Championship Course

Hole	Par	Yards	Hole	Par	Yards
1	4	376	10	4	386
2	4	453	11	3	174
3	4	397	12	4	348
4	4	480	13	4	465
5	5	568	14	5	618
6	4	412	15	4	455
7	4	371	16	4	423
8	3	175	17	4	495
9	4	352	18	4	357
Out	36	3,584	In	36	3,721
			Total	72	7,305

THE OPEN CHAMPIONSHIP
CHAMPIONSHIP
Celebrating 150 Years

Aurum Press
7 Greenland Street, London NW1 0ND

Published 2010 by Aurum Press

Copyright © 2010 R&A Championships Limited

Statistics of the 139th Open Championship produced on an IDS Computer System

Assistance with records and research provided by Malcolm Booth, Alastair Buchan,
Peter Lewis, Salvatore Johnson, and www.golfobserver.com

A CIP catalogue record for this book is available
from the British Library

ISBN-13: 978 1 84513 558 4

Designed and produced by Davis Design
Colour retouching by Luciano Retouching Services, Inc.
Printed in Great Britain by Purbrooks

THE OPEN CHAMPIONSHIP
CHAMPIONSHIP
Celebrating 150 Years

WRITERS
Andy Farrell
John Hopkins
Lewine Mair
Art Spander
Alistair Tait

PHOTOGRAPHERS
Getty Images

David Cannon
Stuart Franklin
Richard Heathcote
Harry How
Ross Kinnaird
Warren Little
Andrew Redington

Scott Halleran
Rob Harborne
Travis Lindquist
Richard Martin-Roberts
Golf Editors

EDITOR
Bev Norwood

The Championship Committee

CHAIRMAN
Michael Brown

DEPUTY CHAIRMAN
Jim McArthur

COMMITTEE

Keith Andrews	Richard Souter
Alick Bisset	Richard Stocks
David Bonsall	Donald Turner
JR Jones	Geoffrey Vero
Stuart Lloyd	David Wybar

CHIEF EXECUTIVE
Peter Dawson

DIRECTOR OF CHAMPIONSHIPS
David Hill

DIRECTOR OF RULES AND EQUIPMENT STANDARDS
David Rickman

Introduction

By Michael Brown

Chairman of the Championship Committee of The R&A

St Andrews Opens are always eagerly awaited but this year's held additional excitement, being the 150th anniversary of the first playing of the Championship at Prestwick in 1860, when the field of eight competed for the Challenge Belt.

The Old Course saw only two changes since the 2005 Open. The decision was taken to encourage play down the right side of the fourth hole by playing from the very back of the existing championship tee for the first time. More significantly, a new tee was introduced at the 17th hole, stretching it by 40 yards and returning the challenge of the second shot to its former and intended severity. Both were a great success.

The Old Course was presented in fantastic condition and for that I must thank Gordon Moir and Gordon McKie and their staff for a tremendous job and for coping with the vagaries of our Scottish summer so well.

Heavy rain marked the middle of the week, and we sadly lost the planned Open Champions' Challenge on the Wednesday to foul weather. Thereafter the Championship was played out in good testing links golf conditions and saw Louis Oosthuisen from South Africa emerge head and shoulders above the field to claim his first Major victory and become the Champion Golfer, playing immaculate golf and displaying great composure in doing so. My congratulations and best wishes to him for what promises to be an exciting future.

My thanks go to the St Andrews Links Trust and their Championship Committee for all their assistance without which the staging of the Championship would not have been possible and also to our thousands of volunteers for their help.

I hope you will find the following pages an enjoyable reminder of a memorable and historic week.

Foreword

By Louis Oosthuizen

To win an Open Championship is special, but to win an Open at St Andrews is something you dream about. Now that it's reality, I can honestly say it is 10 times more than I expected.

I will always remember the scene coming up the last hole. It was an incredible experience. All those people, the noise, the reception and then the silver Claret Jug with my name already engraved was handed over. It was a long time before I let it go and it was the first thing I saw when I woke up the following morning. The party in the Jigger Inn afterwards, the congratulations from my peers, returning home to South Africa — all wonderful memories indelibly etched.

It was fantastic to win on Nelson Mandela's birthday because thoughts of what he had achieved for our country occupied my mind on the walk up the last fairway. I also thought of Ernie Els, whose Foundation gave me the springboard, and Gary Player, whose globe-trotting exploits inspired countless youngsters, plus South Africa's Mr Sport, Johann Rupert.

Last, but always first for me, was my family. Nel–Mare and seven-month-old Jana were there behind the 18th green to share the greatest moment of my sporting life, while my parents were with me in spirit back home. Who knows where it will lead, but nothing will eclipse what happened for me at the Home of Golf.

The Venue

On Golf's Grand Stage

By Andy Farrell

There are Opens, it is said, and then there are St Andrews Opens. There is that touch more anticipation, an added frisson of excitement, and a whole dollop of extra history.

"It may be years before I fully appreciate it," said Tiger Woods shortly after winning his first Claret Jug at St Andrews in 2000, "but I am inclined to believe that winning The Open at the Home of Golf is the ultimate achievement in the sport."

As Peter Alliss has observed, there is nothing to beat visiting the town when it plays host to a big championship, such is the buzz and the tingling atmosphere, unless, of course, it is to return at a quieter time, when the magical aura is no less tangible. The ghosts of golfing greats past haunt every street corner and every sand dune, for all of them have passed this way.

And most, but not all, have triumphed here. Five years ago, Woods became the fifth player to win

two Opens at St Andrews, following Bob Martin, JH Taylor, James Braid, and Jack Nicklaus. Bobby Jones is the only player to have won The Open — in 1927, six years after tearing up his card in disgust — and the Amateur Championship on the Old Course. The latter came in his Grand Slam year of 1930. Other Open Champions here include Sam Snead, Peter Thomson, Bobby Locke, Seve Ballesteros, Nick Faldo, and John Daly. Among those who just missed out were six-time Champion Harry Vardon, the thrilling Arnold Palmer, and the five-time winner Tom Watson.

There could be no grander stage for the 150th Anniversary Open Championship. Obviously, the inaugural Open, and the first 12, took place at Prestwick, where those famous St Andreans Old and Young Tom Morris won eight Opens between them. Young Tom, who tragically preceded his father to the cemetery of the ruined cathedral at the other end of the town, aged only 24, won the original red Moroccan leather belt three times in a row and got to keep it. The Championship was in abeyance for a year (1871) before the Claret Jug was offered as a prize and Young Tom won that, too.

The Swilcan Bridge, with the R&A Clubhouse behind. The 14th hole and Hell bunker (preceding pages).

This year a replica of the Belt was presented to the Champion.

With a history of golf stretching back over 600 years and with The Royal and Ancient Golf Club — founded in 1754 as the Society of St Andrews Golfers — based here, St Andrews has become the spiritual home of the game. No golfers can call themselves the name without teeing up here, the pilgrimage akin to artists visiting Florence and lovers Paris. It seemed natural in 1960 to hold the Centenary Open here and so, too, another half century on.

Like any good home, there is a reassuring air of changelessness. But there are a few differences from 50 years ago. Then Kel Nagle won a first prize of £1,250 out of a total purse of £7,000. By contrast, this year's Champion took home £850,000 out of a pot of £4.8 million. There were fewer grandstands in 1960, the gallery just followed on foot as Palmer mounted a typical, if on this occasion doomed, last-round charge; this year there was seating for 21,500, a record for the Championship. Only six television camera positions captured Nagle's victory, this year every hole was covered in high definition and five miles of fibre-optic cables were buried under the course to provide the most up-to-date communications, including still photographers being able to send pictures directly from the links for the first time. Not so much Royal and Ancient, as ancient and modern.

In golfing terms there is nothing more ancient than the Old Course. It evolved on a narrow strip of land, shaped like a bell hook, between lines of gorse that force shared fairways and over the subtly undulating sand dunes that help form the seven double greens — yet pitted with perilous cavities shaped by the elements, all of which can pound the Fife coast. These became bunkers that offer golfers no shelter at all, quite the opposite. Many are named, but not reassuringly — Mrs Kruger, the Beardies, and, simply, Hell, which is massive. Size is not everything, however. Many, Bernard Darwin wrote, are only big enough for an "angry man and his niblick." Probably his drive looked perfect until his caddie warned, "Mind the wee bunker!" There is *always* a "wee bunker."

It even got to the otherwise saintly Jones, who quit the 1921 Open when he found Hell bunker. He was as frustrated as he had ever been on a golf course, but he was not the first, nor the last, to eventually come to adore the links (Lee Westwood experienced a similar conversion after winning the Alfred Dunhill Links Championship in 2003). "The more I studied the Old Course, the more I loved it," Jones wrote, "and the more I loved it, the more I studied it. There is always a way at St Andrews, although it is not always the obvious

Bunkers known as the Seven Sisters protect the right side of the fairway on the par-5, 568-yard fifth hole.

way." His studies informed the original designs for his own Augusta National.

Unlike modern golfing creations, the Old Course does not signpost its paths of safety or its hazards. Fair? Of course not, but it means there is always a hazard in play no matter the strength or direction of the wind — or even if the course is played backwards (or clockwise) as it routinely was and now is occasionally on 1 April. Only in complete calm is the Old Course susceptible to low scoring, but then any course is in perfect conditions, as Curtis Strange showed with his 62 in the 1987 Dunhill Cup.

Not only is accuracy vital, despite the wide open expanse, but the enduring challenge is finding the safe route, which constantly shifts like the sea. The Auld Lady, wrote Pat Ward-Thomas so evocatively, "can be as tantalising as a beautiful woman, whose smile at once is a temptation and a snare, concealing heartbreak and frustration for some, joy and fulfilment for others, but possession only for the very fortunate few. It does not yield its ancient secrets

lightly or take kindly to contempt and impatience, but it does reward those who give their best in thought, temper, and technique."

Perhaps no one gave more of their best than Woods in 2000. He had just won the US Open by an unprecedented 15 strokes and he would claim The Open by eight with the unthinkable feat of never having gone in a bunker. Clearly, he did not subscribe to the view of Vardon, who complained that the "bunkers are very badly placed" in that they can catch a good drive. The best Vardon did was runner-up in the 1900 Open. What impressed Thomson, who himself plotted his way to victory in 1955 when he twice played out backwards from bunkers on the same hole of the final round, was that Woods did not just pick his line so carefully but hit the ball to the right length every time.

Another from the "plotters" school was Faldo, who relied on notes given to him by Gerald Micklem, a former captain of The Royal and Ancient, listing specific targets on each hole for differing weather conditions. Sadly, Micklem died two years before

The 348-yard 12th hole appears to be an innocuous par 4, but a number of hidden bunkers await.

Faldo triumphed in 1990, but he once said of the Old Course: "It is no use getting cross or trying to do too much. Just cut your losses." Even when Tony Lema won in 1964, after less than two practice rounds, he did so by following to the letter the instructions given to him by Tip Anderson, who otherwise caddied for Palmer at every Open that Palmer played from 1960 to 1995.

It is of some comfort to know that even the best had to rely on local knowledge. Joyce Wethered was the Jones of the women's game and it only took her a couple of holes before surrendering "all claims to independence and delivering myself completely into the hand of my one-armed caddie. For the rest of the round I played obediently over bumps and bunkers, at spires and hotels in the distance, and finally at the 17th hole over the top of a large shed."

The sheds are still there at the 17th, or at least replica ones in front of the Old Course Hotel. The Road Hole was once again the site of drama and controversy after the tee was moved back 40 yards, making the hole play a total of 495 yards. It

had been long suggested that the 17th hole would benefit from additional length. Indeed, in advance of the 1964 St Andrews Open, three-time Open Champion Henry Cotton suggested the alteration: "I would make a tee just beyond the railway line on the other course (he was referring to the Eden Course which is now the practice range). It would restore this drive to its former value..."

Despite this and other recommendations, the change precipitated a furore that brought to mind the words of Raymond Jacobs, in a classic essay from 1990, who was debating the question of whether the Old Course remained an adequate examination for the games of modern professionals. "To alter any of it would be unthinkable; one might as well propose wiping that enigmatic smile from the Mona Lisa," he wrote. "Take out a bunker? Let the rough grow in here? Root out a line of whin bushes there? Introduce a water hazard somewhere? What sacrilegious thoughts."

While some would agree with his assessment, what Jacobs did not know then was that players

Round the Old Course

No 1 Burn • 376 yards Par 4
The widest fairway in golf but the drive needs to be left-centre to avoid the out of bounds on the right. The Swilcan Burn, the only water hazard on the course, runs in front of the green, so the pitch needs to be long even if the flag is forward.

No 2 Dyke • 453 yards Par 4
A blind tee shot that must avoid Cheape's bunker on the left. Anything to the right of it allows for a good angle of attack to the right portion of the course's first, huge double green, which is severely undulating.

No 3 Cartgate (Out) • 397 yards Par 4
Two options: Flirt with the series of pot bunkers on the right and the route to the green opens up. Or take the safer line off the tee over the Principal's Nose on the left, but then the approach is over the mighty crescent-shaped Cartgate bunker in front of the green.

No 4 Ginger Beer • 480 yards Par 4
Again left is safer off the tee but the approach is disguised by mounding in front of the green. Whins on the right have been cleared to encourage more players to go right and improve pace of play on the double fairway. The large bunker slicing into the green on the left of the fourth portion is a no-go area.

No 5 Hole O'Cross (Out) • 568 yards Par 5
The drive must be left of the Seven Sisters, the cluster of bunkers on the right. This is the easier of the two par 5s (the 14th is on the left running in the opposite direction) and most players will get home in two, but if laying up it must be short of the Spectacles bunkers 60 yards short of the green.

No 6 Heathery (Out) • 412 yards Par 4
No margin for error off the tee with bunkers both right and left, the Coffins being the latter and to be avoided as the name suggests. From ideal position this is a good birdie chance with no sand around the green, but the undulating surrounds will still test the short game.

No 7 High (Out) • 371 yards Par 4
A big dogleg right, so the tee shot is aimed to the left of the flag for the 11th green. The green is surrounded by bunkers and Cockle is the large trap short of the green — Tiger Woods drove into it in 2005 but still made a birdie. Marks the start of the "Loop."

No 8 Short • 175 yards Par 3
Out by the Eden Estuary the course now turns back. Might play anything from a long iron to a 9-iron or even wedge depending on the strength and direction of the wind. Must be long to avoid the two bunkers short of the green.

No 9 End • 352 yards Par 4
A short par 4 which is driveable in some wind conditions, otherwise the tee shot must avoid the two bunkers in the middle of the shared fairway with the 10th. A large circular green which is relatively flat, protected by just one bunker short left by the gorse.

No 10 Bobby Jones • 386 yards Par 4
Another shorter par 4, but the fairway narrows at around 280 yards with mounding on the left and the Kruger bunkers on the right. The approach must be carefully controlled due to mounding in front of the green and a putting surface that tilts from front to back.

No 11 High (In) • 174 yards Par 3
A dramatic short hole that puts some bite into the Loop. The front of the green is protected by Hill and Strath bunkers, but the putting surface itself is severely sloped at the front. Vital to leave yourself an uphill putt. Known to some as the shortest par 5 in Scotland.

No 12 Heathery (In) • 348 yards Par 4
Final turn back towards the town and seemingly an innocuous par 4 from the tee. A number of hidden bunkers await in any wind condition, while the green is the shallowest on the course and has some severe slopes so the pitch-and-run approach must be judged perfectly.

No 13 Hole O'Cross (In) • 465 yards Par 4
The drive must take on the Coffins in the right-centre of the fairway, and there is no prospect of running up an approach so the second must fly all the way onto the green. Unlike most of the double greens the 13th green is long rather than wide.

No 14 Long • 618 yards Par 5
As testing a drive as they come, with out of bounds on the right and the Beardies on the left. No wonder the ideal landing area is called the Elysian Fields. The second shot must avoid the huge trap that is Hell by going down the left, leaving a short pitch to the "table-top" green.

No 15 Cartgate (In) • 455 yards Par 4
Sutherland, a nasty pot bunker at 260 yards, must be avoided off the tee, but the main threat is the green itself which appears deceptively close and large. Distance control is the key here, plus avoiding bunkers front and back.

No 16 Corner of the Dyke • 423 yards Par 4
Another classic hole with options. Take on the out of bounds on the right and the approach is more straightforward. Go left of the Principal's Nose bunker on the safe line and two bunkers up by the green come into play for the second.

No 17 Road • 495 yards Par 4
Newly extended by 40 yards to restore the difficulty of the tee shot. The blind drive, over the sheds and grounds of the hotel, will have to be farther left than of late, bringing the infamous Road Hole bunker more into play on the second shot. Often a chip-and-putt par is the best option from either short right or left by the 18th tee.

No 18 Tom Morris • 357 yards Par 4
Back to the relative safety of the first fairway, the line off the tee is the clock on the R&A Clubhouse to avoid the out of bounds on the right. But from the left the approach must clear the Valley of Sin, the magnetic hollow in front of the green, to find a pin that is never far from this danger.

The Old Course Hotel stands alongside the 17th, which was extended by 40 yards, with a new tee on the other side of the path.

Lowest Scores On Old Course In The Open

88	Tom Kidd	1873
86	Bob Martin	1876
86	Davie Strath	1876
84	Jamie Anderson	1879
84	Jamie Allan	1879
83	Bob Ferguson	1882
83	Archie Simpson	1885
83	Hugh Kirkaldy	1891
83	Hugh Kirkaldy	1891
83	John Ball Jr	1891
77	Sandy Herd	1895
75	JH Taylor	1900
71	Willie Smith	1910
71	George Duncan	1910
70	Jock Hutchinson	1921
68	Bobby Jones	1927
68	Walter Hagen	1933
68	Abe Mitchell	1933
68	Craig Wood	1933
67	Dai Rees	1946
67	John Fallon	1955
67	Laurie Ayton Jr	1957
67	Eric Brown	1957
67	John Fallon	1957
66	Bernard Hunt	1960
66	Jack Nicklaus	1964
65	Neil Coles	1970
63	Paul Broadhurst	1990
63	Rory McIlroy	2010

would one day hit the ball so far that on the 17th they would require as little as an 8-iron for their second shot at a hole which, while still worthy of respect, was no longer the absolute terror of yore. Remember, Watson went over the green onto the road with a 2-iron in 1984, a crucial mistake, while ahead Ballesteros was making the winning birdie at the 18th.

It was that year in an earlier round that Ballesteros, summarising his play, talked through the 17th thus: "A good tee shot, 5-iron, chip, two putts for a par-5." George Simms, the press officer, corrected the Spaniard, saying the hole was a par 4. "For you, George, it may be a par 4. For Seve Ballesteros, it is a par 5!"

This was the first increase in length of the Road Hole for over 100 years. Back in the day, it was presumably played as a three-shotter. The point is the terror of the 17th dovetails with the relative ease of the 18th — eight strokes for the two remains the paradigm, a classic illustration of the phrase "level 4s."

Over the centuries, man has made many changes to the God-given golf course. Old Tom Morris did most to shape land into what we know today and, though no one would dare dump a water hazard out there, whins have indeed been cut back and most of the bunkers date from only a century ago. A number of new tees were created for the 2000 and 2005 Opens, when the weather was about as kind as it could be to the best players in the world, but the 17th was the only hole to be lengthened this time. Like any home, changes are inevitable but are quickly absorbed by the Old Course. What is changeless is the St Andrews experience, as timeless and magical as ever.

Exempt Competitors

Name, Country	Category
Thomas Aiken, South Africa	5
Robert Allenby, Australia	6, 7, 20
Byeong-Hun An*, South Korea	30
Fredrik Andersson Hed, Sweden	9
Ricky Barnes**, USA	6
Jason Bohn, USA	17
Angel Cabrera, Argentina	6, 12, 13, 16, 20
Mark Calcavecchia, USA	1
Alejandro Canizares, Spain	11
Paul Casey, England	6, 7, 8
KJ Choi, South Korea	6
Stewart Cink, USA	1, 2, 4, 5, 6, 16, 20
Tim Clark, South Africa	6, 15, 20
Darren Clarke, Northern Ireland	11
Ben Crane, USA	6
Ben Curtis, USA	1, 2, 4
John Daly, USA	1
Rhys Davies, Wales	9
Jason Day**, Australia	6
Luke Donald, England	5, 6, 16
Victor Dubuisson*, France	31
Jason Dufner, USA	16
David Duval, USA	1, 2
Simon Dyson, England	7
Ernie Els, South Africa	1, 2, 4, 5, 6, 7, 16, 20
Sir Nick Faldo, England	1
Gonzalo Fernandez-Castano, Spain	7
Ross Fisher, England	6, 7
Rickie Fowler, USA	6
Jim Furyk, USA	6, 16, 20
Stephen Gallacher, Scotland	10
Sergio Garcia, Spain	6, 7, 15
Brian Gay, USA	16
Lucas Glover, USA	6, 12, 16, 20
Mathew Goggin, Australia	5
Retief Goosen, South Africa	5, 6, 7, 16, 20
Paul Goydos, USA	19
Bill Haas, USA	17
Todd Hamilton, USA	1, 2
Anders Hansen, Denmark	7, 23
Soren Hansen, Denmark	5, 7
Peter Hanson, Sweden	6, 7
Padraig Harrington, Republic of Ireland	1, 2, 4, 6, 7, 14, 16
Gregory Havret, France	10
JB Holmes, USA	17
Yuta Ikeda, Japan	6
Trevor Immelman, South Africa	13
Ryo Ishikawa, Japan	6, 20
Thongchai Jaidee, Thailand	6, 7, 21
Jin Jeong*, South Korea	29
Miguel Angel Jimenez, Spain	6, 7, 8
Dustin Johnson, USA	6, 16
Richard S Johnson, Sweden	5
Zach Johnson, USA	6, 13, 16, 20
Robert Karlsson, Sweden	6
Martin Kaymer, Germany	6, 7
Jerry Kelly, USA	16
Simon Khan, England	8
Kyung-tae Kim, South Korea	27
Soren Kjeldsen, Denmark	7
Matt Kuchar, USA	6
Paul Lawrie, Scotland	1
Tom Lehman, USA	1
Marc Leishman, Australia	16
Justin Leonard, USA	1, 5, 20
Thomas Levet, France	7
Davis Love III**, USA	6
Sandy Lyle, Scotland	1
Hunter Mahan, USA	6, 16, 20
Steve Marino, USA	16
Graeme McDowell, Northern Ireland	6, 12
Ross McGowan, England	7
Rory McIlroy, Northern Ireland	6, 7
Phil Mickelson, USA	6, 13, 14, 16, 20
Katsumasa Miyamoto, Japan	27
Hirofumi Miyase, Japan	26
Edoardo Molinari, Italy	6
Francesco Molinari, Italy	6, 7
Ryan Moore, USA	19
Kevin Na, USA	6, 16
Alexander Noren, Sweden	7
Koumei Oda, Japan	25
Ryuichi Oda, Japan	24
Geoff Ogilvy, Australia	6, 7, 12, 16, 20
Sean O'Hair, USA	6, 16, 20
Mark O'Meara, USA	1
Louis Oosthuizen, South Africa	6
Jeff Overton, USA	6
Jae-Bum Park, South Korea	26
Kenny Perry, USA	6, 16, 20
Ian Poulter, England	6, 7
Alvaro Quiros, Spain	6, 7
Loren Roberts, USA	28
Robert Rock, England	7
Justin Rose, England	18
Charl Schwartzel, South Africa	6, 7
Adam Scott, Australia	6, 20

Name, Country	Category	Name, Country	Category
John Senden, Australia	16	Nick Watney, USA	6, 16
Michael Sim, Australia	6, 22	Bubba Watson, USA	18
Vijay Singh, Fiji	20	Tom Watson, USA	1, 4, 5
Heath Slocum, USA	16	Mike Weir, Canada	16, 20
Shunsuke Sonoda, Japan	26	Lee Westwood, England	5, 6, 7
Henrik Stenson, Sweden	6, 7, 15	Oliver Wilson, England	6, 7
Steve Stricker, USA	6, 16, 20	Chris Wood, England	5
Toru Taniguchi, Japan	26	Tiger Woods, USA	1, 2, 4, 6, 12, 14, 16, 20
Scott Verplank, USA	16	YE Yang, South Korea	6, 14, 16, 20
Camilo Villegas, Colombia	6, 7, 20		

* Denotes amateurs   **Denotes reserves

Key to Exemptions from Regional, Local Final and International Final Qualifying

Exemptions for 2010 were granted to the following:

(1)   Past Open Champions aged 60 or under on 18 July 2010.

(2)   The Open Champions for 2000-2009.

(3)   Past Open Champions born between 17 July 1944 and 19 July 1948.

(4)   Past Open Champions finishing in the first 10 and tying for 10th place in The Open Championship 2005-2009.

(5)   First 10 and anyone tying for 10th place in the 2009 Open Championship at Turnberry.

(6)   The first 50 players on the Official World Golf Ranking for Week 21, 2010, publication date Monday 24 May 2010.

(7)   First 30 in the final European Tour Order of Merit for 2009.

(8)   The BMW PGA Championship winners for 2008-2010.

(9)   First 3 and anyone tying for 3rd place, not otherwise exempt, in the top 20 of the Race to Dubai for 2010 on completion of the 2010 BMW PGA Championship.

(10)   First 2 European Tour members and any European Tour members tying for 2nd place, not otherwise exempt, in a cumulative money list taken from all official PGA European Tour events from the Official World Golf Ranking for Week 19 up to and including the BMW International and including The US Open.

(11)   The leading player, not otherwise exempt, in the first 5 and ties of each of the 2010 Open de France ALSTOM and the 2010 Barclays Scottish Open. Ties will be decided by the better final round score and, if still tied, by the better third round score and then by the better second round score. If still tied, a hole by hole card playoff will take place starting at the 18th hole of the final round.

(12)   The US Open Champions for 2006-2010.

(13)   The US Masters Champions for 2006-2010.

(14)   The US PGA Champions for 2005-2009.

(15)   The PLAYERS Champions for 2008-2010.

(16)   The leading 30 qualifiers for the 2009 TOUR CHAMPIONSHIP.

(17)   First 3 and anyone tying for 3rd place, not exempt having applied (6) above, in the top 20 of the PGA TOUR FedExCup Points List for 2010 on completion of the HP Byron Nelson Championship.

(18)   First 2 PGA TOUR members and any PGA TOUR members tying for 2nd place, not exempt, in a cumulative money list taken from the PGA TOUR PLAYERS Championship and the five PGA TOUR events leading up to and including the 2010 AT&T National.

(19)   The leading player, not exempt having applied (18) above, in the first 5 and ties of each of the 2010 AT&T National and the 2010 John Deere Classic. Ties will be decided by the better final round score and, if still tied, by the better third round score and then by the better second round score. If still tied, a hole by hole card playoff will take place starting at the 18th hole of the final round.

(20)   Playing members of the 2009 Presidents Cup teams.

(21)   First and anyone tying for 1st place on the Order of Merit of the Asian Tour for 2009.

(22)   First and anyone tying for 1st place on the Order of Merit of the Tour of Australasia for 2009.

(23)   First and anyone tying for 1st place on the Order of Merit of the Southern Africa PGA Sunshine Tour for 2009.

(24)   The Japan Open Champion for 2009.

(25)   First 2 and anyone tying for 2nd place, not exempt, on the Official Money List of the Japan Golf Tour for 2009.

(26)   The leading 4 players, not exempt, in the 2010 Mizuno Open Yomiuri Classic. Ties will be decided by the better final round score and, if still tied, by the better third round score and then by the better second round score. If still tied, a hole by hole card playoff will take place starting at the 18th hole of the final round.

(27)   First 2 and anyone tying for 2nd place, not exempt having applied (26) above, in a cumulative money list taken from all official 2010 Japan Golf Tour events up to and including the 2010 Mizuno Open Yomiuri Classic.

(28)   The Senior Open Champion for 2009.

(29)   The Amateur Champion for 2010.

(30)   The US Amateur Champion for 2009.

(31)   The European Amateur Champion for 2009.

(29) to (31) were only applicable if the entrant concerned was still an amateur on 15 July 2010.

Local Final Qualifying
29 June

Fairmont St Andrews
Laurie Canter*, England	69 67	136
Zane Scotland, England	66 71	137
Mark F Haastrup, Denmark	69 69	139

Kingsbarns Links
Colm Moriarty, Ireland	67 70	137
Jamie Abbott*(P), England	70 70	140
Tom Whitehouse(P), England	71 69	140

Ladybank
Tyrrell Hatton*, England	67 69	136
Phillip Archer, England	66 70	136
Simon Edwards(P), England	71 66	137

Scotscraig
Paul Streeter, England	69 66	135
Gary Clark(P), England	68 69	137
Steven Tiley(P), England	69 68	137

* Denotes amateurs   (P)Qualified after playoff

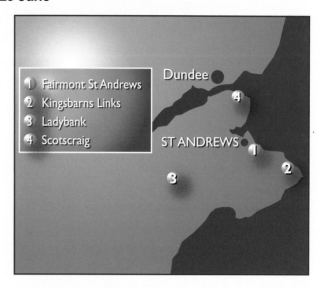

1 Fairmont St Andrews
2 Kingsbarns Links
3 Ladybank
4 Scotscraig

Dundee

ST ANDREWS

The Starting Field

"G. In the event of an exempt player withdrawing from the Championship or further places becoming available in the starting field after the close of entries, these places will be allocated in the ranking order of entrants from OWGR (Official World Golf Ranking) at the time that intimation of withdrawal is received or further places are made available by the Championship Committee. Any withdrawals following issue of OWGR Week 27 will be taken in ranking order from OWGR Week 27."

Ricky Barnes, USA, replaced David Toms, USA
Davis Love III, USA, replaced Anthony Kim, USA
Jason Day, Australia, replaced Greg Norman, Australia

Phillip Archer

Laurie Canter

Gary Clark

Zane Scotland

International Final Qualifying

ASIA
10 & 11 March

Saujana   *Malaysia*

Hiroyuki Fujita, Japan	67	66	133
Danny Chia, Malaysia	66	68	134
Seung-Yul Noh, South Korea	66	68	134
Eric Chun*, South Korea	67	71	138

*Denotes amateur

Hiroyuki Fujita

AMERICA
24 May

Gleneagles   *Plano, Texas*

Tim Petrovic, USA	64	65	129
Bo Van Pelt, USA	65	65	130
DA Points, USA	63	68	131
Martin Laird, Scotland	69	63	132
Tom Pernice Jr, USA	64	69	133
Glen Day, USA	67	67	134
George McNeill, USA	68	66	134
Cameron Percy(P), Australia	68	67	135

(P) Qualified after playoff

Tim Petrovic

AUSTRALASIA
14 & 15 January

Kingston Heath   *Melbourne, Australia*

Kurt Barnes, Australia	70	64	134
Ewan Porter, Australia	68	68	136
Peter Senior, Australia	69	70	139

Kurt Barnes

EUROPE   7 June

Sunningdale   *Berkshire, England*

Shane Lowry, Rep of Ireland	62	67	129
Andrew Coltart, Scotland	66	65	131
Colin Montgomerie, Scotland	69	62	131
Gareth Maybin, N Ireland	64	68	132
Thomas Bjorn, Denmark	65	67	132
Jose Manuel Lara, Spain	66	67	133
Tano Goya, Argentina	66	67	133
Ignacio Garrido, Spain	64	69	133
Bradley Dredge, Wales	68	65	133
Marcel Siem(P), Germany	64	70	134

(P) Qualified after playoff

Shane Lowry

St Andrews ★

AFRICA   20 & 21 January

Royal Johannesburg & Kensington   *Johannesburg, South Africa*

Darren Fichardt, South Africa	67	69	136
Jean Hugo, South Africa	65	71	136
Josh Cunliffe(P), South Africa	70	68	138

(P) Qualified after playoff

Darren Fichardt

McIlroy Makes Hay and History

By Andy Farrell

Records fell on a surprisingly calm morning as Rory McIlroy led a procession of 73 under-par scorers.

If there is always great anticipation for any St Andrews Open, like Christmas coming round only every five years, then the 150th anniversary version of golf's oldest and grandest championship certainly lived up to the expectations. On what turned into a record-breaking opening round, the golf was often exciting, never less than intriguing, from the moment Paul Lawrie, the 1999 Champion, hit the first ball on the Old Course.

Most dramatic of all was Rory McIlroy's 63, a nine-under-par effort that gave the young Northern Irishman a two-stroke lead over South Africa's Louis Oosthuizen. John Daly, the 1995 Champion, was among an eclectic group of five players on six under par, while Tiger Woods, the Champion at St Andrews in 2000 and 2005, and Lee Westwood

One under par after eight, Rory McIlroy played the next 10 holes in eight under.

headed the group on 67. It was the first time Woods had not led an Open round on the Old Course since the first round in 2000, when he also had a 67 but Ernie Els had a 66.

Of course, scoring at St Andrews is regulated by the weather and after two relatively mild Opens here it was obvious this year would be different. The previous Sunday's practice round was hit by winds of 50mph and it was so wet, windy, and generally miserable on Wednesday that the Champions' Challenge had to be cancelled. That evening a haunting haar gripped the town, but a bigger danger to play starting on time the following morning was the return of heavy rain overnight. It finally stopped at 4am and the greenkeeping staff went into action immediately to ensure The Open started promptly at 6.30am.

What the morning players found when they opened their curtains was a delightful surprise. There might have been the odd bit of rain, and a dank oppression hung in the air, but it was flat calm. With the course soft after all the rain and not a breath of wind the Old Course was ripe for low scoring. "John Daly was seven under after 11,

For the first time in memory, past Champions led off the first two rounds, with Paul Lawrie having the honour on Thursday.

so you thought someone was going to do it," Padraig Harrington said of McIlroy's runaway start. The Dubliner added: "But you don't need to look at the leaderboards, you just know the scoring is going to be good here with ideal conditions."

While Daly showed what was possible, it was McIlroy who took advantage. His 63 not only equalled the lowest round in a Major Championship, but was the lowest ever in the first round of The Open. He went past the previous best by a stroke with a birdie at the last. "It was a fantastic score," he said. "It was great to get into the rhythm of the round and into a flow. It was a very pleasant round of golf."

McIlroy's excitement about playing in his first Open at St Andrews was more than youthful exuberance. The winner of the Silver Medal as leading amateur at Carnoustie in 2007 grew up playing the great links of Northern Ireland such as Royal Portrush

and Royal County Down. He was also buoyed by his compatriot Graeme McDowell winning the US Open at Pebble Beach a month earlier. "I always thought my game needed a further two or three or four years of development and that a Major was further away than it probably is," the 21-year-old explained. "But seeing Graeme win at Pebble made me realise that it might not be as far away as I thought it was."

McDowell put it rather more bluntly: "Rory told me he does not want to be the only Irishman at the Ryder Cup without a Major Championship."

But where McIlroy's dreams and the expectations of some of the game's more flinty-hearted observers found common accord was in the empirical evidence of his past outings on the Old Course. He had played two rounds as an amateur in the St Andrews Links Trophy with scores of 69 and 69, and then, after turning professional, six rounds in the

First Round Leaders

HOLE	1	2	3	4	5	6	7	8	9	10	11	12	13	14	15	16	17	18	
PAR	4	4	4	4	5	4	4	3	4	4	3	4	4	5	4	4	4	4	TOTAL
Rory McIlroy	4	4	(3)	4	5	4	4	3	(2)	(3)	(2)	(3)	4	(4)	(3)	4	4	(3)	63
Louis Oosthuizen	4	4	4	(3)	(4)	4	(3)	(2)	(3)	(3)	3	4	4	(4)	(3)	4	[5]	4	65
John Daly	(3)	(3)	4	4	5	(3)	4	(2)	(3)	(3)	(2)	4	4	5	4	4	[5]	4	66
Andrw Coltart	4	4	4	4	(4)	(3)	4	3	(3)	(3)	[4]	4	4	(4)	(3)	4	4	(3)	66
Steven Tiley	(3)	4	4	4	(4)	(3)	4	3	(3)	4	3	4	(3)	5	(3)	4	4	4	66
Bradley Dredge	(3)	4	(3)	4	(4)	4	4	3	4	(3)	3	4	4	(4)	4	4	4	(3)	66
Peter Hanson	4	(3)	(3)	4	(4)	4	4	3	4	(3)	[4]	4	4	5	(3)	4	(3)	(3)	66

Champions' Challenge

The R&A donated The Open Champions' Challenge prize fund of £50,000 to the Seve Ballesteros Foundation. The prize was due to be awarded to the winning team in the Champions' Challenge, but the event was cancelled due to adverse weather conditions.

Tuesday night, at the Champions Dinner, the Past Champions who were due to compete in Wednesday's event agreed that the winning team would award the prize money to Seve's charity. The R&A had made the sum available for the team of Champions that won the Challenge to give to a charity of their choice.

The Foundation aims to channel funds into ongoing research, particularly into brain cancer, the condition with which Ballesteros was diagnosed in October 2008. It also aims to support young golfers with limited economic resources to develop their career in the game.

Ballesteros had planned to attend the 150th Anniversary Open Championship and intended to play in the Champions' Challenge. In June, however, he was advised by his doctors against making the trip to St Andrews.

Teeing off on the 18th, Louis Oosthuizen finished with 65, two behind the leader.

An afternoon starter, Bradley Dredge returned a 66 with two halves of 33.

Peter Hanson birdied the last two for 66.

Alfred Dunhill Links Championship: 67, 68, 68, 67, 65, 69. "I've played so well around here before that I really felt if I could come into this Championship with good form I'd have a great chance," he said.

Nothing in his first practice rounds on the Old Course on the Friday and Saturday before the Championship, nor his last the previous morning when he had gone out at the crack of dawn and was back having breakfast in the Old Course Hotel before the worst of the weather which meant most players could not complete a full round, had dissuaded McIlroy from thinking his ninth competitive round on the Old Course would be anything other than in the 60s again.

Yet there was little indication that it would capture the day's headlines. He birdied the third from 12 feet but was still one under leaving the eighth green. "Going to the seventh I said to myself that I could still turn in 33 and get going from there," McIlroy said. "I was able to do that and just kicked on from there." He managed it with an eagle-2 at the 352-yard ninth where he drove to 15 feet and holed the putt. By coming home in 30 it meant he played the last 10 holes in eight under par.

He birdied the next three holes, then the par-5 14th and the 15th to be eight under heading to the 17th, the Road Hole. Back in 2007 in the final round of the Dunhill Links, McIlroy hit a 6-iron to three feet and holed the putt for a birdie that helped secure his European Tour card after just two events as a professional. Now, despite the hole being lengthened by 40 yards, he again had a 6-iron for his second shot which he hit to three feet. It was a stroke of brilliance to underline why he is one

Andrew Coltart posted a 66 with birdies on three of the last five holes.

The R&A Clubhouse was reflected off casual water after heavy overnight rain.

"Bleary-eyed Paul Lawrie got up with the birds then fired some late birdies as his Open challenge finally woke up after a slow start."

—**Euan McLean,** *Daily Record*

"The early starters in The Open awakened as if in a dream Thursday, to a still, soft morning with a light misting rain. If this really was St Andrews, and that really was the Old Course sitting out there defenceless, wrapped up in a ribbon for the taking, then it was time to make a move or get out of the way."

—**Larry Dorman,** *The New York Times*

"Genius declared itself at the earliest opportunity yesterday as Rory McIlroy, 21 years old with a savant's touch, played himself to the top of the leaderboard after the opening round of the 2010 Open Championship."

—**Lawrence Donegan,** *The Guardian*

"Perhaps Tiger Woods should try a stint working for the Beeb. Andrew Coltart put on the headphones at the 2009 Open and was so inspired by watching Tom Watson that he qualified for St Andrews this year and shot a 66 in yesterday's opening round."

—**Mark Reason,** *The Daily Telegraph*

"'Twas a strange and fascinating Thursday, this opening round of the 150th Anniversary Open. The past and future trumped the present."

—**Bill Dwyre,** *Los Angeles Times*

Nick Watney's 67 included five birdies and no bogeys.

Lucas Glover returned a 67 while watching Rory McIlroy's 63.

of the most talented and exciting youngsters in the game, and there are a few to choose from at the moment.

"It went through my mind on 17 that 62 would have been the lowest round in a Major," he admitted. "That's probably why I missed the putt." Birdies at the last two holes would have given him a 62. But after the disappointment of 17, he collected himself to make sure of the 3 at the 18th, pitching to three feet and holing that one. "The birdie at 18 made up for the miss on 17," he said. "I don't think I can come off feeling let down. I'm leading The Open Championship. It would have been lovely to shoot 62, but I can't complain."

A birdie on the 18th resulted in a 67 for YE Yang.

Fredrik Andersson Hed finished 5-3 for his 67.

He became the 22nd player to score a 63 in a Major Championship, which has now been achieved on 24 occasions. Eight of those were in The Open, but only once previously had it been done at St Andrews, by Paul Broadhurst in the third round in 1990. Broadhurst, at 25, was the previous youngest man to do it. McIlroy, at 21, became the third youngest player in modern times to lead a Major after the first round — Seve Ballesteros, at the 1976 Open, and Sergio Garcia, at the 1999 US PGA Championship, were both 19. As for winning Majors, Seve was 22 when he won at Lytham in 1979, Woods was 21 when he claimed the 1997 Masters. But should McIlroy go on to win, he would be the youngest winner of The Open since Willie Auchterlonie, who was less than a month past his 21st birthday, in 1893.

Of course, Young Tom Morris was 17 when he won for the first time in 1868. While no one had ever before scored lower than 64 in an 18-hole opening round of The Open, there is a case to say that the best *ever* start to an Open was Young Tom's 47 at 12-hole Prest-

First Round Scores	
Players Under Par	73
Players At Par	23
Players Over Par	60

"You get the feeling that what's in John Daly's head looks like his pants: a lot of swirls, a lot of clashing hues. But it's just possible that the most extreme thing about Daly these days is his clothing. His huge gut is gone, and he claims to be sober. Excess means settling for paisley."

—**Sally Jenkins,** *The Washington Post*

"Players always talk about getting on the wrong side of the draw at The Open, fearing a shift in conditions so drastic that fields can be split in two in the blink of an eye. That was not quite the case yesterday."

—**Peter Dixon,** *The Times*

"What's been lost in John Daly's career is the level of his natural talent. Few players have ever possessed the combination of extraordinary power and touch that Daly had in his prime."

—**Ron Green Jr,**
The Charlotte Observer

"Stewart Cink blew the chance to get his Open defence off to a flier — despite enjoying the best of the conditions. The 37-year-old American carded 70 to finish the first round seven shots off the pace."

—**Jim Black,** *The Sun*

"A brash youth mugged a defenceless old lady here yesterday, but at least left her with a shred of dignity."

—**James Corrigan,** *The Independent*

John Daly, with a 66, was seven under par after 11 holes.

wick in 1870. It included a 3 at the first hole, measuring 578 yards, and he went on to win by 12 strokes, winning for the third time in succession, retaining forever the original Challenge Belt, and setting a record of 149 which was never beaten in the further 20 years the Championship was played over 36 holes. To collect a replica of the Belt which would be presented to the new Champion on Sunday, McIlroy would have to become St Andrews' first first-time Major winner since Tony Lema in 1964.

McIlroy is no stranger to low scoring. Five years earlier as a 16-year-

The 'Mild' Thing Now?

John Daly's Tale of Highlights and Heartbreak

The manufacturer is called Loudmouth Golf Apparel, and the attire it creates, trousers showing swirls of paisley prints or tiger stripes, speaks volumes. John Daly calls them his "good luck pants," while others glance at the kaleidoscopic patterns and merely sigh, "Good luck." Which, dressed to the nines, an appropriate phrase for golf, is what Daly had for a few hours at the 150th Anniversary Open Championship in the return to what he calls "my favourite course in the world." Also a great many good shots.

That his opening-day 66 would be diminished by three subsequent less distinguished rounds did nothing to alter Daly's viewpoint on clothing. Or the public's viewpoint on Daly, who despite all his troubles, the gambling losses, the dissipation, the divorces, remains remarkably popular. And intensely candid.

"I have never run from my mistakes," said Daly. "I've always been honest with you guys (in the media)."

Daly's tale is one of highlights and heartbreak, earning him two Major victories, that stunning 1991 PGA Championship when he arrived as the ninth alternate and the 2005 Open at St Andrews, and an unenviable reputation.

There was too much drinking. There were broken marriages. There were busted-up hotel rooms. "The Wild Thing," he was nicknamed, as much for his inability often to control his life as to control his tee shots.

His was a talent squandered, a career of missed opportunities, of angered sponsors, and disillusioned friends. Jack Nicklaus, in the time before Tiger Woods, predicted Daly would win multiple Masters. But in 12 appearances at Augusta, a course that should have surrendered to his blend of power and touch, his best finish is third place.

Daly's world further disintegrated in 2007 and 2008. He smashed a tee shot off the top of a beer can during a pro-am. At another tournament, he returned from a rain delay

with the then Tampa Bay Buccaneers gridiron coach as his caddie. He was shown in a memorable photo in an orange jail suit, eyes half-closed. The combination drew a suspension from the PGA Tour for the opening half of 2009.

His weight at nearly 400 pounds, Daly in February 2009 underwent gastric lapband surgery. The drinking stopped. "I can no longer tolerate beer or junk food," said Daly. The weight dropped more than a hundred pounds. He survives on Cokes. And cigarettes.

"I'm 44 years old," said Daly after the fine first round, "and I've learned a lot. … I've screwed up a lot in my life, but it's how you come back and deal with it that counts. I'm not out of it. I'm still in it."

Daly, perhaps now to be identified as "The Mild Thing" — other than his attire — said there is an advantage to his trousers. "The good thing is you get dressed in the dark and any shirt is going to match."

—Art Spander

Low Scores	
Low First Nine	
Sean O'Hair	30
Low Second Nine	
Rory McIlroy	30
Low Round	
Rory McIlroy	63

With 32 on the outward nine, Marcel Siem posted a 67 including a birdie at the 18th.

Ryo Ishikawa returned a 68.

Ian Poulter (left) posted a 71 and Ernie Els, 69, in a featured group.

old he set the course record at Portrush with a 61, while earlier in the season he won for the first time on the PGA Tour in America with a closing round of 62 at the Quail Hollow Championship. "It is hard to compare," he said. "The 61 at Portrush was probably slightly better and I was buzzed to do a score like that for the first time on a course with such a great reputation.

"But this is probably more special because it is at St Andrews and it's The Open Championship. I love the course and it fits my eye really well. You have to be so inventive, it's a lot of fun to play. If I had one course to play, this would be it. But you definitely needed to take advantage of the conditions. We have had so much rain and going out there this morning with no wind, you're never going to get St Andrews playing any easier."

As it was the 150th Anniversary Open, it was fitting that a former Champion led the way. Lawrie hit a hybrid down the first fairway and posted a 69. "It was a lovely morning out there," he said. If it was overcast and grey, then Daly's pastel-splodged trousers bright-

Graeme McDowell, 71, went out in 37.

One under after four, Tiger Woods was smiling as he completed a 67.

In the **Words** of the **Competitors...**

"

"It's a good score (68). I played really good. I didn't miss many shots at all, so I was expecting a little better."

—Robert Rock

"For the real golfers this was for the taking. Fortunately for me, it makes it playable."

—Sir Nick Faldo

"It's to me my favourite golf course all over the world that I have ever played."

—John Daly

"It was a nice lovely morning out there, despite the early start."

—Paul Lawrie

"With the conditions we had, you had to go get it. You had to take advantage of it. I felt like I did a pretty good job of that today."

—Tiger Woods

"I did all the superfluous things very well and I did the important things badly."

—Padraig Harrington

"That's the vagaries of golf. You don't always have it."

—Justin Rose

"

ened things up. "They're kind of like my good luck start pants," he said. He was another former Champion out very early and, following the trend of recent good opening rounds, he birdied the first two holes. Then he added five more in six holes from the sixth to top the leaderboard.

"He was driving it great and looked very calm," reported playing companion Andrew Coltart. "This place suits the long hitters. He could attack some of the pins with his lob wedge, while I was hitting in 5-iron." Coltart matched Daly's 66 and was enjoying a renaissance of his own. It was not long ago he had missed 16 cuts in a row. He had not played in an Open since 2002 and the last two he had only been inside the ropes as a radio commentator for BBC Five Live.

Coltart birdied three of the last five holes, but Daly missed at least four chances to improve on his score. Then he went onto the gravel path behind the 17th green and dropped a shot. At his press interview afterwards, the 44-year-old former "Wild Thing" said: "I think this is the first time I've seen the media centre at the British Open since 1995. It's a good feeling. I've got a lot of memories here. But someone will beat 66 today. It's a matter of making some putts. The greens are not really fast but they are rolling great. I'm not a

Phil Mickelson's 73 included a double-bogey on the 13th.

Padraig Harrington, on 73, started by pitching into the burn.

firm putter and that's why I missed those putts down the stretch."

Woods arrived at St Andrews in his attempt to become the first player to win three Opens on the Old Course and promptly changed his putter. Out went the Scotty Cameron which he had used for 11 years and in winning 13 of his 14 Major titles, in came a similar Nike model which he said was more suitable for slower greens. "I am pleased with it," Woods said after returning a 67. "It comes off the face faster and these greens are the slowest I've seen in a long time. It came off well and I putted pretty good."

Out in 33, Woods made three birdies in a row from the 12th to get to six under but bogeyed the 17th and failed to birdie the last. Playing in a tournament overseas for the first time since the scandal that engulfed his private life in the winter, Woods was received warmly and seemed well placed to improve on his previous two Major outings when he tied for fourth at both the Masters and the US Open.

Playing alongside Woods was Justin Rose, one of the form players entering the Championship. Rose had just won two out of three events on the PGA Tour to earn his place at St Andrews for the first time. In 2005 it had been particularly frustrating when he was first

Round of the Day

OFFICIAL SCORECARD
THE OPEN CHAMPIONSHIP 2010
THE OLD COURSE, ST ANDREWS

FOR R&A USE ONLY 112

ROUND 1
18 HOLE TOTAL

Rory MCILROY
Game 11
Thursday 15 July at 8:20am

THIS ROUND __63__   __63__

VERIFIED __117.__

ROUND 1

Hole	1	2	3	4	5	6	7	8	9	Out	10	11	12	13	14	15	16	17	18	In	Total
Yards	376	453	397	480	568	412	371	175	352	3584	386	174	348	465	618	455	423	495	357	3721	7305
Par	4	4	4	4	5	4	4	3	4	36	4	3	4	4	5	4	4	4	4	36	72
Score	4	4	3	4	5	4	4	3	2	33	3	2	3	4	4	3	4	4	3	30	63

Signature of Marker

Signature of Competitor — Rory McIlroy

The key to Rory McIlroy's 63, which tied The Open and Major records, was his eagle-2 on the ninth, when McIlroy drove the green on the 352-yard hole and rolled in a 15-foot putt. "I was one under through eight holes," McIlroy said, "and then the eagle on nine really sort of turned things around for me, and I just got going from there.

"I was actually trying to go left of the two bunkers in the middle of the (ninth) fairway but pushed it a little bit, and hit it well enough that I was able to carry the bunkers."

Yet, at the other side of his round, was "one I let get away." It was the difficult 17th, the Road Hole, and McIlroy struck his second shot with a 6-iron to three feet from the hole, which he thought was his "most enjoyable" stroke of the round. But McIlroy missed the three-footer and rather than have a chance at 62, he needed a birdie-3 from three feet on the final hole for his 63. "It went through my mind on 17 that 62 would have been the lowest round in a Major," he said. "That's probably why I missed the putt."

Between, McIlroy birdied the 10th with a wedge shot to six feet, the 11th with a 7-iron to eight feet, and the 12th from four feet after driving the green. He chipped to 10 feet and birdied the 14th, and birdied the 15th after a 9-iron to 15 feet.

reserve and sat on the first tee all day but never got a chance to play. This time he birdied the first two holes, but a 70 for him and a 71 for Ian Poulter represented disappointing returns in the conditions.

Harrington's 73, compiled in the group just after Woods and Rose, was even more deflating for the two-time Champion. He pitched into the Swilcan Burn with his second shot at the first and never got going after that. With typical honesty, he said: "I did all the superfluous things very well and I did the important things badly." Another visitor to the Swilcan Burn was Oliver Wilson, who drove into it to become the only player all week to miss the biggest opening fairway in the world. Wilson did recover to post a 68.

Amateur Champion Jin Jeong started with a 68.

Round One Hole Summary

HOLE	PAR	YARDS	EAGLES	BIRDIES	PARS	BOGEYS	D.BOGEYS	HIGHER	RANK	AVERAGE
1	4	376	0	36	104	13	3	0	11	3.89
2	4	453	0	25	88	39	3	1	5	4.15
3	4	397	0	30	115	11	0	0	13	3.88
4	4	480	0	10	111	29	6	0	3	4.20
5	5	568	4	77	65	10	0	0	18	4.52
6	4	412	0	27	109	16	3	1	9	3.99
7	4	371	0	35	106	14	1	0	14	3.88
8	3	175	0	10	121	23	2	0	7	3.11
9	4	352	1	60	91	4	0	0	17	3.63
OUT	**36**	**3,584**	**5**	**310**	**910**	**159**	**18**	**2**		**35.24**
10	4	386	0	30	117	6	3	0	12	3.88
11	3	174	0	11	114	31	0	0	6	3.13
12	4	348	1	32	105	17	0	1	10	3.91
13	4	465	0	17	99	36	4	0	4	4.17
14	5	618	0	62	71	22	1	0	16	4.76
15	4	455	0	18	109	29	0	0	8	4.07
16	4	423	0	8	111	32	4	1	2	4.22
17	4	495	0	5	76	56	16	3	1	4.60
18	4	357	1	43	105	6	1	0	15	3.76
IN	**36**	**3,721**	**2**	**226**	**907**	**235**	**29**	**5**		**36.51**
TOTAL	**72**	**7,305**	**7**	**536**	**1,817**	**394**	**47**	**7**		**71.75**

Steve Stricker's 71 featured two birdies and a bogey.

Although 73 players broke par, a record in Majors for the opening round, the importance of going out early could be seen from the fact that 34 of the first 54 players (the first 18 groups) broke par but only 39 of the last 102 players. The scoring average for the morning was over two strokes lower than for the afternoon starters when the wind picked up.

Prominent among the later groups were Westwood, who produced an impressive 67 with five birdies in a row from the fifth. Paul Casey, suffering from a sore throat, had a 69, but McDowell returned a 71, Luke Donald a 73, Phil Mickelson also a 73 with a double-bogey at the 13th and his only birdie at the last, and Colin Montgomerie a 74. The Ryder Cup captain drove out of bounds into the hotel at the 17th, then found the Road Hole bunker before getting up and down from the treacherous sand trap for a double-bogey. The day's worst horror story at the hole came from Anders Hansen, who

Steven Tiley's 66 was the best of 21 Englishmen in the field.

Lee Westwood, 67, had an outward 31.

Sean O'Hair posted 30-37–67.

Justin Rose, 70, started with two birdies.

took four to get out of the bunker in a quadruple-bogey-8 before chipping in for an eagle at the last.

Westwood was playing with a strained plantaris muscle in his right calf. The injury had flared up at the French Open, when he initially feared it might be deep vein thrombosis. A scan and subsequent treatment revealed that, while rest was the best solution, he could do no more harm by continuing to play and he was not about to miss The Open. Before going off for further treatment after the round, he said: "It was tricky out there. This morning was a piece of cake, you could kick it round in a decent score. I expected someone to shoot a 62 for the first time today. We got a little bit unlucky with the weather, but we might get a break tomorrow."

While Bradley Dredge, the Welshman chasing a Ryder Cup appearance on home soil later in the year, and Sweden's Peter Hanson joined the group on 66, the most striking name on six under was that of Steven Tiley. Striking because it was virtually unknown. The 27-year-old journeyman professional from Kent went off in the middle of the day and returned the best score of any of the 21 Englishmen in the field, many of them prominent on the World Ranking.

Like McIlroy, Oosthuizen had missed the cut in the first two Majors of the year. Unlike McIlroy, who had already recorded three top-20

"They came, they saw and eventually Steven Tiley did England proud. While all the pre-game talk centred on the classiness of the group of Englishmen coming into this Open, it was left to the one chap no one knew about to fly the flag for much of yesterday's opening round."

—**Bill Elliott,** *The Guardian*

"If there was a single heckler of fallen hero Tiger Woods yesterday, I didn't hear it; and if there was a tantrum from the world number one, I missed that too."

—**Douglas Lowe,** *The Herald*

"Three of the six Scots in the field were left to rue problems they encountered at the Road Hole. While Paul Lawrie, Andrew Coltart and Martin Laird all negotiated the most famous hole in golf without a tale to tell, the same couldn't be said of Stephen Gallacher, Sandy Lyle or Colin Montgomerie."

—**Martin Dempster,** *The Scotsman*

"Trust Rory McIlroy to be the one to mark this landmark anniversary of The Open Championship with a performance for the ages. Nobody has ever felt more at home at the Home of Golf than the 21-year-old Ulsterman, but even by his standards this was memorable."

—**Derek Lawrenson,** *Daily Mail*

"Phil Mickelson's Open hopes were badly dented by a disappointing 73."

—**James Nursey,** *Daily Mirror*

Sergio Garcia chipped onto the 17th and saved par-4 in his 71.

finishes in Major Championships, Oosthuizen had made the cut only once in his eight previous appearances and never in his three previous Opens. Also, he had only broken par once in a Major before this 65, compiled early in the afternoon just two groups after Tiley. It was still calm as the 27-year-old South African played the outward nine and he collected six birdies in seven holes from the fourth.

Instead of practising in the wet of Wednesday, Oosthuizen headed indoors to The R&A Swingzone and played Tri-Golf with the youngsters gathered there. He enjoyed the afternoon and finished fourth behind Bill Haas in the special pro challenge. Back to more important matters and, although he had won the Open de Andalucia in March for his maiden title on the European Tour, recent missed cuts had been disappointing.

After consulting sports psychologist Karl Morris, Oosthuizen put a red dot below the thumb on the glove he wears on his left hand. The idea was to trigger a pre-shot routine every time he looked down at his glove. "I have the ability to get away from the game, especially when it is slow play," he explained. "I think of all kinds of things. But it is hard for me to get back into the moment. Looking at the dot is my trigger to forget about everything else and focus on the next shot."

Although he missed the cut at the Barclays Scottish Open, Oosthuizen felt the change was working. One other change he had been

Louis Oosthuizen
A Humble Man, Full of Passion

Thanks to Rory McIlroy and his 63, Louis Oosthuizen was able to stay nicely under the radar with his opening 65. Others might have felt a little miffed at the relative lack of interest in what was a seven-under-par tally, but not Oosthuizen.

"He has always been a very modest man," explained Gary Player. "He's got plenty of passion in there but he is endlessly humble, always respectful of others."

Player had enjoyed a round with his 27-year-old compatriot at Augusta in April and noted then that he was driving the ball as far as any of the game's more famously long hitters.

Intriguingly, Oosthuizen's caddie, Zack Rasego, had once been "Caddie of the Year" on a caddie programme that Player had set up at Sun City in South Africa. Part of the prize had been to carry Player's bag during a stint on the European Tour, and Rasego had made the maximum of the opportunity. "He was a quick learner and someone who had a good eye for his job," Player said.

Oosthuizen joined the European Tour in 2004 following an amateur career in

which he was indebted to the Ernie Els Foundation. "But for the Foundation," he said, "I wouldn't have been here." Over three years, it helped with his travel and tournament expenses, while Els himself served as the best of mentors.

The confidence which was missing from Oosthuizen's first few years in Europe first started to seep into his play in 2009 when he notched a couple of second-place finishes on the so-called Desert Swing. Then, at the start of 2010, it came with a rush as he captured the Open de Andalucia. He could not wait to take the trophy home to show his wife, but he carried it no farther than Malaga Airport, where it was deemed a "dangerous object" and confiscated by

Monarch Airlines.

On the first day at St Andrews, Oosthuizen had no more dangerous implement in his bag than his putter. He was holing from everywhere as he sped to the turn in 31.

"I think," he said, with delicious understatement, "I can read these greens." In fairness, he knew their contours from seven appearances in the Dunhill Links Championship.

As Oosthuizen posted his 65, there were those who checked on his record to see if there was any indication to suggest that he could be shaping to win the Claret Jug. The punters did not exactly rush to put their money on him. Though he had captured an Irish and an Indian amateur championship and bagged four titles on the South African Tour in addition to his Open de Andalucia title, his Open history was less than impressive. It took in four failed attempts to qualify and three missed cuts.

Surely not the stuff of a Major Champion in the making?

—Lewine Mair

thinking about was his caddie, Zack Rasego, who had been with him since 2003. During Monday's practice round he told Rasego that this would likely be their last week together. With that out in the open, the birdies would not stop coming. He had a 4 at the 14th and a 3 at the 15th — by now the wind was blowing hard — to threaten McIlroy's lead. But he bogeyed the 17th and settled for seven under.

Like McIlroy, Oosthuizen is no stranger to low scores, although nothing can beat the 57 on his home course of Mossel Bay back in 2002. "I shot a 65 once in the Dunhill Links, but this is the first time I've played in an Open here," he said.

Jim Furyk, ranked fifth in the world, struggled to a 77.

HOLE	PAR	PLAYER	SCORE	CUML
18	-9	McILROY	63	
16	-8	OOSTHUIZEN		
18	-6	DALY	66	
18	-6	COLTART	66	
16	-6	TILEY		
18	-5	ANDERSSON HED	67	
18	-5	WOODS	67	
18	-5	SIEM	67	
18	-5	GLOVER	67	
18	-5	WATNEY	67	
18	-5	O'HAIR	67	
18	-5	CANIZARES	67	

Under-par scores were the rule beneath Hamilton Hall.

Tom Watson posted a 73 on his return to the Old Course.

After 6 on the 17th, Colin Montgomerie trudged home with 74.

"It's holy ground we are walking on. The win in Malaga earlier in the year got my confidence going, but recently, though I'd been playing well, I just hadn't been making any putts. Today I made a few." Indeed, nobody had fewer than his 27.

Should either McIlroy, who beat the South African head-to-head in the final round of the Dubai Desert Classic in 2009, or Oosthuizen go on and win they would set a new record for the lowest opening score by a Champion. But there was a long way to go before any Champion would be crowned and the forecast for Friday was for high winds. "I've never actually played St Andrews when the weather is bad," said McIlroy. "That's probably why my scores have been quite good. I wouldn't mind it blowing a bit as long as it stays dry."

Tom Watson, now 60 and a year on from his valiant attempt to snag a sixth Claret Jug at Turnberry, had some colourful imagery to describe the day. "The Auld Lady didn't have any clothes on today," Watson said after a 73. "What she gave away this morning, she will take back the next three days. It will be a wonderful test of golf."

THE FIRST DAY, BUT WHAT A DAY

By Alistair Tait

Rory McIlroy doesn't need much inspiration when he arrives in St Andrews. The young Northern Irish player loves the Old Course, but he turned up for the 150th Anniversary Open Championship with an extra spring in his step.

Graeme McDowell was the man responsible for raising McIlroy's spirits.

McIlroy has been pegged as a star since he was in short trousers. From the day he was old enough to make a passable swing at a little white ball, he has seemed destined to stand at the very pinnacle of world golf. After all, he was hitting 40-yard drives when he was two years old. At eight he became the youngest full member of Holywood Golf Club, five miles east of Belfast. At nine he won the World Championship Under-10 at Doral in Florida. At the same age he appeared on the Gerry Kelly Show, a popular Irish programme, where he chipped nine balls out of 10 into a washing machine. At 11 he shot level par round Holywood's par-69 layout. Two years later and his handicap was down to scratch.

He played in his first professional event, the 2005 British Masters, at age 15. He won both the West of Ireland and the Irish Amateur Close Championships that year, and smashed the course record at Royal Portrush with an 11-under-par 61 in the North of Ireland Amateur.

He announced himself to the wider world in the 2007 Open Championship at Carnoustie with the way he played the opening round. His bogey-free 68 proved he could play on the world stage. It came as no surprise when he took just two tournaments to gain his European Tour player's card at the end of 2007. A third-place finish in the lucrative Alfred Dunhill Championship at St Andrews gave him his Tour ticket.

The 21-year-old has lived up to expectations ever since. His first European Tour victory came in the 2009 Dubai Desert Classic. He chased Lee Westwood all the way that year to become European number one, just missing out in the final event to end the year as European number two.

He began the 2010 season by taking his first PGA Tour win when he blew the field away in the Quail Hollow Championship in Charlotte, North Carolina, a final-round 62 putting an emphatic seal on the win. He arrived at St Andrews as the world's ninth-ranked player. No wonder the bookmakers had him listed at 16-1 to win.

McIlroy pulled out of the Barclays Scottish Open the week before to prepare for The Open. More importantly, a round of golf with

Graeme McDowell at Royal County Down shortly after McDowell captured the US Open gave McIlroy faith that he could win at the Home of Golf.

"Graeme's win definitely gave me a lot of belief and a lot of confidence knowing if he can go out and win a Major the way he did, there's no reason why I can't go out and have good chances to win," McIlroy said. "I always thought a Major was a little further away than it probably is. I always thought

maybe another two or three or four years of development in my game, I'd be ready to challenge for Majors. But seeing Graeme win at Pebble Beach made me realise that it might not be as far away as I thought it was."

It certainly didn't seem that far away considering the way he played the first round. McIlroy started his Open campaign slowly. He was one under par by the time he reached the ninth tee, a 3 at the par-4 third hole a meagre return considering the way he was playing.

Then he caught fire. He drove the green at the par-4 ninth, rolling the ball to 15 feet from the flag on the 352-yard hole. He drained the putt and that set off a chain reaction. Birdies followed at the 10th, 11th, 12th, 14th, 15th, and 18th holes. When he holed out on the 18th, McIlroy became the 23rd player in Major Championship history to shoot 63. It could have been better. He missed a three-foot birdie putt on the 17th green that would have put him in a class of his own.

"It went through my mind on 17 that 62 would have been the lowest round in a Major. That's probably why I missed the putt," McIlroy said. "I don't think I can come off feeling let down. I'm leading The Open Championship. But yeah, definitely the one on 17 was one I let get away."

McIlroy did much to lift the spirits of the large galleries on a drab, wet morning. His score would hold throughout the day, giving him a two-shot lead over Louis Oosthuizen.

St Andrews expected as much of him. Surely the gifted one was about to fulfil all the headlines written about him.

If the crowds were getting carried away, then McIlroy wasn't. "I really felt that if I could come into this golf tournament in good form and playing well, I feel as if I've got a great chance," McIlroy said before adding the important caveat. "It's only the first day, and there's 54 holes left to play. I can't really be thinking about that (winning), to be honest."

Watson Departs at Twilight

By Andy Farrell

In times as different as day and night, a young South African took his first Open lead and a five-time Champion bid farewell to St Andrews.

For those spectators who stayed right to the end of golf's longest day, and even some who may have slipped away for dinner but were drawn back to the late-night action, the second day's play of the 150th Anniversary Open provided a fitting climax. The scene at the 18th hole of the Old Course, perhaps the most famous setting in the game, crackled with excitement and nostalgia. First, Tiger Woods very nearly holed his drive for an albatross, then Tom Watson said his farewell to St Andrews in the time-honoured fashion.

All this was happening at nearly 10pm, many hours after Louis Oosthuizen had taken the lead in The Open for good — around 8am — and following an afternoon of buffeting winds that caused a suspen-

sion in play for over an hour and a suspension in the good scoring of earlier in the Championship. It was a day of survival and Woods arrived at the final tee two over par for his round. With a swing that showed confidence in his driving was returning following the split from former coach Hank Haney, Tiger set the ball off parallel with Gibson Place, the road to the right of the fairway, and then saw it break left on landing, almost clattering into the flagstick as it passed inches from the hole.

He faced a good eagle chance but had to settle for a birdie to get back to four under par, some eight strokes behind Oosthuizen's halfway lead at 12 under. As Woods, Justin Rose, and Camilo Villegas were about to putt on the green, they stood aside to let the threesome behind of Watson, Padraig Harrington, and Ryo Ishikawa tee-off before the hooter sounded to halt play for the night. By now dusk had well and truly fallen and at 9.45pm the klaxon sounded — players were entitled to finish the hole they were on.

Watson marched towards the bridge over the Swilcan Burn, leant down and kissed the ancient stonework. Then he jumped up onto the bridge and

Tom Watson said this was not his last Open Championship, but his last at St Andrews.

Teeing off at the fifth in a sea of umbrellas, Miguel Angel Jimenez returned a 67 for a total of 139.

waved to the gallery behind the 17th green, all the way up the road by the 18th, those hanging out of the windows of the houses overlooking the course, and the hardy souls still in the stand behind the final green. The lights in the R&A Clubhouse blazed, but nightfall added an intimacy to the poignant farewell.

"I thought of Arnold on the bridge, I thought of Jack on the bridge," Watson said. "Their last Opens were right here at St Andrews. This is not my last Open Championship. I intend to play some more. But it's my last Open Championship at St Andrews." Watson never won an Open at the Home of Golf, although he came close in 1984. "There's no regret, none at all," he said. "I had my opportunities here and didn't make the best of them."

Few players have formed such a mutual bond of respect with The Open gallery as the five-time Champion. "I think the main thing was the respect I have for the way the game is played over here, the respect that the people have for their game," Watson said. "The Scots invented golf and they love the game with a passion unlike any other people. I enjoy that."

Watson faced a chip shot over the Valley of Sin and very nearly holed it. One more roll and it would have dropped in. "Is this a gimme?" Watson asked the gallery before tapping it in. A 75 left the 60-year-old at four over par and missing the cut. There would be no repeat of the heroics of a year earlier at Turnberry, where he almost landed a sixth Claret Jug in true fairytale fashion before losing to Stewart Cink in a playoff. A change in the exemption regulations by The R&A now allows

Louis Oosthuizen missed this putt on 17, but his 67 produced a five-shot lead.

Excerpts FROM THE Press

"'If it's nae rain and noe wind, then it's nae gowf.' So goes the old Scottish refrain. Well, there was nae rain for most of Friday's play at the Old Course, but there was plenty of gowf. The menu offered a buffet, a smorgasbord, of weird happenings as players, buffeted by the whipping winds, tried to cope."

—Lorne Rubenstein,
***The Globe and Mail*, Toronto**

"When Paul Casey drove on the left side of the Road Hole, he suspected a very good round was about to be downgraded to a merely satisfactory 69. He took two thrashes to get out of the long stuff, which did not please him as he complained later. 'It is far too thick,' he said. Which is a very good reason not to go anywhere near it, of course."

—Kevin Mitchell, *The Guardian*

"Nobody does misery quite like Colin Montgomerie, whether it is huddling under a brolly in the rain or twiddling his putter like a cheerleader's baton in frustration at a missed opportunity on the 18th."

—Mike Dickson, *Daily Mail*

"Eleven years, countless missed opportunities in the Major Championships and more than his share of putting torment have combined to get the better of Sergio Garcia since that moment at the 1999 PGA Championship when he announced himself as the next big thing."

—Paul Forsyth, *The Scotsman*

Second Round Leaders

HOLE	1	2	3	4	5	6	7	8	9	10	11	12	13	14	15	16	17	18	TOTAL
PAR	4	4	4	4	5	4	4	3	4	4	3	4	4	5	4	4	4	4	TOTAL
Louis Oosthuizen	4	4	4	4	4	3	3	3	4	3	4	3	5	4	4	4	4	3	67-132
Mark Calcavecchia	4	4	4	3	4	4	4	3	4	4	2	3	4	5	4	4	4	3	67-137
Paul Casey	3	3	3	4	5	3	4	2	4	4	3	4	4	5	4	4	7	3	69-138
Lee Westwood	4	4	4	4	4	4	4	3	4	4	3	4	4	5	4	4	4	4	71-138
Jin Jeong*	4	4	4	4	4	4	3	4	4	4	3	4	4	4	5	4	4	3	70-138
Alejandro Canizares	4	4	3	4	4	5	4	3	4	5	3	4	4	5	4	4	4	3	71-138
Tom Lehman	4	4	4	4	5	4	4	2	4	4	3	3	4	4	4	4	4	3	68-139
Ricky Barnes	3	4	4	4	3	4	3	3	4	3	3	4	4	7	5	4	5	4	71-139
Peter Hanson	4	5	4	4	4	4	3	3	4	4	4	4	3	5	4	5	5	4	73-139
Miguel Angel Jimenez	3	3	3	5	4	4	3	3	3	4	4	4	5	5	3	3	4	4	67-139
Graeme McDowell	3	4	5	5	4	4	3	2	3	4	3	5	4	5	4	3	4	3	68-139
Retief Goosen	4	4	4	4	4	3	4	3	3	4	4	4	4	5	4	4	4	4	70-139
Sean O'Hair	5	5	4	4	4	4	4	4	3	4	3	4	4	5	4	4	3	4	72-139

*Denotes amateur

Low Scores

Low First Nine

Paul Casey	31
Miguel Angel Jimenez	31

Low Second Nine

Mark Calcavecchia	33
Tom Lehman	33

Low Round

Louis Oosthuizen	67
Mark Calcavecchia	67
Miguel Angel Jimenez	67
Rickie Fowler	67

a former Champion who finishes in the top 10 in any year, instead of bowing out at 60, to play for another five years. Watson has four more years, through to Hoylake in 2014, but The Open will not return to St Andrews until 2015 at the earliest.

On the Tuesday of Open week, Watson had received an honorary doctorate from the University of St Andrews along with Arnold Palmer and Padraig Harrington. Watson said at the ceremony that Palmer had always been his idol and the reason he had beaten Jack Nicklaus all those times was to make up for the times Nicklaus had beaten Palmer. Now, like Nicklaus, Watson exited the Old Course with a birdie at the last, but it had been a punishing round.

"This golf course was tough today," Watson said. "I said yesterday she was naked, but she put on her boxing gloves today and hit us with all she had. I had a lot of fun playing it." Fun was not the universal sentiment around the locker room, but that is why Watson was always different. He was asked if Carnoustie, venue for The Senior Open Championship the following week, would seem easy after this. "Give me a break," he laughed. "Carnoustie is never easy."

While Watson departed, there were a couple of 50-year-old Americans high on the leaderboard. Tom Lehman, the 1996 Champion, had a 68 to be five under for the Championship, while Mark Calcavecchia, who was victorious at Royal Troon in 1989, had a 67 to be seven under. They both played early in the morning, Calcavecchia earlier than anyone else. Like Paul Lawrie the day before, he was given the

Paul Casey had a 69 for 138, the only blemish a 7 on the Road Hole.

Alejandro Canizares joined the group on 138 with a 71, including a birdie at 18.

With 17 pars and one birdie for a 71, Lee Westwood felt he 'didn't get as much out of my round as I should have.'

Rickie Fowler followed a 79 with a 67 to make the cut.

honour of hitting the first tee shot of the second round at 6.30am.

It turned out to be the best time to play this Friday. There was some heavy rain at times but the wind had not worked up to full blast yet. Calcavecchia was out in 34, back in 33 with a birdie at the 18th, and did not drop a shot. The opening group finished a good half hour in front of the field. At seven under, Calcavecchia was still two strokes behind the overnight leader, Rory McIlroy, who would not be going out until the afternoon. But he was also now five behind the new man at the top of the leaderboard, Oosthuizen.

The 27-year-old South African was in the day's second group and also scored a 67. Added to his opening 65, he tied the record for halfway in a St Andrews Open of 132 set by Nick Faldo and Greg Norman in 1990. The day did not start well. Oosthuizen was on the range with his coach, Pete

Round of the Day

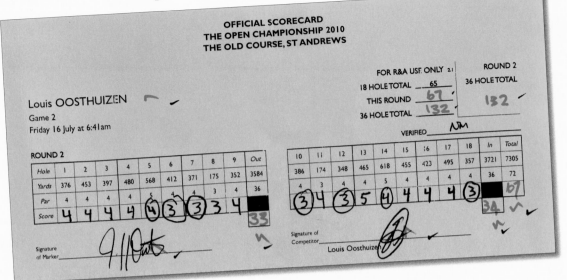

OFFICIAL SCORECARD
THE OPEN CHAMPIONSHIP 2010
THE OLD COURSE, ST ANDREWS

Louis OOSTHUIZEN
Game 2
Friday 16 July at 6.41am

FOR R&A U.S.F. ONLY 2.1
18 HOLE TOTAL ___65___
THIS ROUND ___67___
36 HOLE TOTAL ___132___

ROUND 2
36 HOLE TOTAL ___132___

VERIFIED ___NJM___

ROUND 2

Hole	1	2	3	4	5	6	7	8	9	Out
Yards	376	453	397	480	568	412	371	175	352	3584
Par	4	4	4	4	5	4	4	3	4	36
Score	4	4	4	4	4	3	3	3	4	33

	10	11	12	13	14	15	16	17	18	In	Total
	386	174	348	465	618	455	423	495	357	3721	7305
	4	3	4	5	5	4	4	4	4	36	72
	3	4	3	5	4	4	4	4	3	34	67

Signature of Marker

Signature of Competitor
Louis Oosthuizen

In the group with the second tee time at 6.41am, Louis Oosthuizen found conditions that were not ideal for low scoring, with rain and wind at the outset, then just wind, then rain and wind again through his first 13 holes. But Oosthuizen, who posted a 65 in the first round, managed to be three under par to that point in his round. He finished with birdies on the 14th and 18th holes. His was one of four 67s on the day.

"When we started off, we had the bad wind, because the front nine was tough," Oosthuizen said. "From the second hole to the seventh hole was really tough. The rain stopped. The wind was still up, though, and we got to 10 and it started raining again. And then the wind just dropped completely, and from 14 we had the last five holes downwind, which is a huge difference.

"If we played the front-nine wind on 14, it was probably a good three-shot hole, and I was hitting a 5-wood in there today."

Oosthuizen posted three consecutive birdies from the fifth. He chipped his third shot to five feet on the par-5 fifth. He had a two-putt birdie from 50 feet on the sixth and holed a 15-foot putt on the seventh. He scored birdies on the 10th, 12th, and 14th holes, but dropped shots on the 11th and 13th. He drove the 10th green, chipped to three feet on the 12th, and two-putted the par-5 14th.

Cowen, at 5.30am. His caddie, Zack Rasego, and bag of clubs were not. Rasego, having overslept, finally arrived at 6.10, half-an-hour prior to his tee time. Oosthuizen, rather than bawling out his caddie as many would have done, calmly warmed up with a few wedges, a few mid-irons, and a few drivers and then headed for the first tee, the incident forgotten.

The rain had started by the time Oosthuizen birdied the fifth to get to eight under. He then birdied the sixth to go level with McIlroy and then the seventh, where he holed from 15 feet, to take the lead at 10 under par. A run of three birdies and two bogeys from the 10th left him at 11 under, and after driving the green at the last,

INFORMATION

PLAY SUSPENDED DUE TO HIGH WIND

THE OPEN
www.opengolf.com

Scorers were posting higher numbers on the second day.

Aged 50, Mark Calcavecchia posted a 67 to hold second place, saying: 'It doesn't matter how old you are.'

Sir Nick Faldo was out after an 81.

he two-putted for a seventh birdie of the day to reach 12 under. He led then by three from McIlroy but would end the day five ahead of Calcavecchia, who had moved up to second place.

"It's probably the position anyone wants to be in playing a Major at a weekend," the South African said. "It's what we work to achieve. I'm just happy with the two rounds I have put together." It was only the second time in nine Majors that Oosthuizen was going to play on the weekend, let alone be at the top of the leaderboard. By now everyone wanted to know more about him. At 54 on the World Ranking, his name was hardly unknown, just unpronounceable.

"You've got to at least learn to pronounce his name if he is leading The Open Championship," joked compatriot Trevor Immelman. It is WUHST-hy-zen, apparently, for those who can get their tongues round the Afrikaner vowels. Born Lodewicus Theodorus, he has always been known as Louis, until friends anointed him "Shrek" after the loveable ogre due to the gap in his teeth. His father, a farmer, wanted him to play tennis at first, but later converted himself once his sons had the golf bug.

Past Champions Have the Honour

Have The R&A no thought for the elderly? In what they later said was a tribute to former Champions, the organisers required Mark Calcavecchia, winner of The Open at Royal Troon in 1989, to hit the first ball on Friday. A 4.30am alarm call to be ready for a 6.30am tee time. Is this what a man just past his 50th birthday and Brenda, his wife and caddie, really wanted? Apparently, yes.

"I'm an early riser anyway, so I'll play at 6.30 any day," said Calcavecchia, who was competing in his 24th Open. "The R&A is nice enough to know that I like to play fast and they certainly know I'm not going to hold anybody up. But that was the first time I actually hit first. It was pretty cool, actually."

Not only did Calcavecchia have the benefit of playing the course without anyone in front of him, he caught it at its most benign, which it most certainly was not at 2.40pm when play was halted for over an hour because strong winds were causing balls to move on the more exposed parts of the course. By then, Calcavecchia was home, his 67 giving him a two-round total of seven under par, which looked better the longer the day went on. At the end, he was alone in second place.

The 1999 Champion, Paul Lawrie, aged 41, had the honour on Thursday and returned a 69 but went home after an 82 in the second round. After playing his last 10 holes of the first round in four under, Lawrie had a double-bogey and eight bogeys on Friday.

Calcavecchia's score was one of four 67s, the lowest round of the day, and the American said he had been inspired by Tom Watson's performance in The Open the previous year. "It doesn't matter how old you are. I think old guys can hang with the young guys."

It was a reminder that while Calcavecchia may have arthritis in his knuckles and he needs a fatter grip on his putter to help take the tension out of his hands, and he likes a beer or two after a round, he can still play good golf.

"You know when you're 30, your parents are 50 and you're like 'How can anybody be that old?'" he said. "But now that you're that age you don't really think about what you were thinking about when you were 30. I haven't grown up anyway. I'm still 30. I may feel 50 or 60, but inside I'm still 30."

He had eagled the 17th in the first round, a rare score on that hole. There were no such eagles in his second round, just 13 pars, no bunkers or three-putts, and five birdies. Down the years Calcavecchia and his putters have had a turbulent relationship — he once carried two in his bag — but on this day the instrument and its master were on good terms.

—**John Hopkins**

He hails from Mossel Bay. They say at the golf club there you can see the sea from every hole. They say of the town that even the seagulls walk. It's a windy place. No matter that Oosthuizen got some favourable tee times compared to others, he can flat out play in the wind. "The front nine was tough, with heavy rains at times," he said. "But then the wind dropped, and then from 14 it picked up again but was behind, so that was a huge difference."

Oosthuizen was done by midday and would have a long wait for his third round. With a seven-month-old baby daughter, Jana, and wife Nel-Mare for company he would have plenty to do to take his mind off the golf. "Jana will definitely occupy me for the next day," he said. "And we'll probably watch some of the golf."

It was a wild watch the rest of the day. Compared to Thursday, the average score went up by

The 1996 Champion, Tom Lehman, had a 68 to be in the top 10.

"The walls of the Dunvegan Hotel, which sits a block from the 18th green, is covered with pictures and memorabilia from bygone Championships at the Old Course. One in particular tells you how strongly the locals feel about the most defining feature of their links gem. It's of Tiger Woods in 2000, with his record-setting scores typed neatly underneath: 67-66-67-69–269. Scribbled right next to it in an indignant hand are the words, 'No Wind.'"

—Scott Michaux, *Augusta Chronicle*

"Respect. That is what Rory McIlroy learned yesterday. Respect for a course that he had boxed about the ears on his nine previous meetings. Respect for a game that appeared effortless on the opening day."

—Kevin Garside, *The Daily Telegraph*

"Mark Calcavecchia won The Open an eon ago, back in 1989, when he was in his prime. Now, he is 50. He has arthritic knuckles. He's headed from the Old Course here up the road to Carnoustie next week, where he will play in The Senior Open Championship. But for the second straight year, Calcavecchia is playing well in The Open."

—Barry Srvluga, *The Washington Post*

"Louis Oosthuizen must have felt like the man who won the lottery yesterday — largely because he was."

—Neil Squires, *Daily Express*

Retief Goosen went out in 33, finished with a 70 and tied for seventh.

three strokes to over 74. While there were 73 under-par rounds on day one, there were 26 in round two. And of those 26, three were not recorded until Saturday morning from the 30 players who were unable to finish their rounds on Friday night. Of the other 23, they were all compiled early in the day, the last of them a 71 by Martin Kaymer who teed-off in the 17th group of the day at 9.31am.

Notable among those early scores were two more 67s from Miguel Angel Jimenez, who joined Lehman at five under, as did US Open champion Graeme McDowell with a 68, while the other 67 came from Rickie Fowler. The young American rookie had opened with a 79 so he got it back to two over par — at the time he finished he was about four strokes off the cut line so he had to wait until the next morning to discover that he was in exactly on the number.

England's Lee Westwood and Paul Casey both got to the clubhouse at six under, Westwood after a solid 71 and Casey after a second successive 69. Both might have been better placed. Westwood had not been able to practise the previous week due to his calf injury and felt a slight rustiness to his game might have cost him four strokes. Casey gave three strokes back at the Road Hole due to a 7. He drove into the thick rough on the left and then had an air shot. "I was going sideways, so I couldn't go at it too hard, otherwise I

Robert Karlsson had a 71 despite a double-bogey on the 13th.

could have ended up in room 312 of the hotel," he said. "The club just went straight underneath it." For his third he actually aimed back down the fairway and then his fourth came up short of the green and he took three putts to get down.

It was a sign of the impending carnage that neither man was too unhappy at his position. Granted they could do nothing about the six-shot deficit to the leader until the following day, but at least they did not have to go out in the worst of the wind. Woods and Rose teed-off at 2.20pm and both three-putted the first green. "It was blowing so hard, our putts were impossible," Tiger said. "Rosey's putt wasn't a bad putt, but the wind got it and it went 18 feet left of the hole." The dropped shot put Woods on course for a 73, his first round over par in an Open at St Andrews since 1995 when he was a amateur.

It was at 2.40pm, just after Woods and Rose cleared the first green, that officials suspended play. By now there had been numerous instances of balls

Graeme McDowell posted a 68 with birdies on 16 and 18.

Three birdies and two bogeys left Ignacio Garrido on 140 after a 71.

After going five under through 10 holes, Ricky Barnes posted a 71, and was four over on the last five.

Peter Hanson was on 139, with 73 despite bogeys on 16 and 17.

moving on the greens, especially out at the loop. The meteorologists on site reported gusts out on the most exposed part of the course at over 40mph. "A number of greens became unplayable," said David Rickman, The R&A's Director of Rules and Equipment Standards. "We had problems at the 12th, 13th, 10th, 11th, and seventh, those out at the far end of the course by the estuary. We had a series of incidents in close succession of balls moving."

The delay lasted for 65 minutes. The last time play was suspended in The Open was at Royal Birkdale in 1998 when winds gusting to over 50mph and the threat of lightning in the Irish Sea briefly brought play to a halt on the second afternoon. Ironically, given that The Open was celebrating its 150th anniversary, rounds were washed out due to rain at both the Silver Jubilee and Centenary Opens in 1910 and 1960.

Naturally, many players were not happy campers. Some of those who had just finished complained that they had had to play on, so why not those currently out on the course? Those whose rounds got interrupted complained that conditions were exactly the same when they got back out to restart

Another First for Asia
South Korea's Jin Jeong Is Low Amateur

South Korea's Jin Jeong only had limited experience of links golf when he turned up for The Open Championship. It wasn't obvious from his opening two rounds.

When Jeong returned a second round of 70, two under par, to go with his opening 68 to stand at six under par, he recorded another historic feat. He was guaranteed to become the first Asian to win the Silver Medal as low amateur, just a month after becoming the first Asian winner of the Amateur Championship. He was the last man standing of the seven amateurs in the field, the only one to make the cut. More impressively, he was only six shots off the lead.

The 20-year-old had never seen a links growing up in Busan, South Korea. Jeong arrived at The Open as a permanent resident of Australia. He moved there when he was aged 17 to work with Trevor Flakemore at Waverley Golf Club near Melbourne. Flakemore caddied for Jeong at St Andrews. He is responsible for turning Jeong into a golfer with a bright future.

Jeong first tasted seaside golf at Glasgow Gailes when he finished seventh in the Scottish Stroke Play Championship. His first St Andrews experience didn't signal what was to come in The Open. He missed the cut in the St Andrews Links Trophy because he couldn't handle the Jubilee Course. However, he did get a practice round on the Old Course and fell in love with it. Maybe that's what inspired him to win the Amateur Championship and qualify for The Open. Jeong blew the field away at Muirfield, defeating Scotland's James Byrne 5&4 in the 36-hole final.

"I didn't like it the first time," Jeong said about his introduction to links golf. "When I play in the US or Australia I can control the ball, but here the ball bounces everywhere. I couldn't do anything around the greens. Most times I hit it over the green. I couldn't spin the ball on the greens. Now I love it."

If Jeong had belief after the Amateur, he gained even more after playing practice rounds for The Open. He learned he could keep up with the world's best. He hit drives past Davis Love III and country-

man YE Yang. The latter blow went on his Facebook page, a feat he said made it "the happiest day of my life."

"It's a dream come true," Jeong said about playing in The Open. "I played the Amateur and finally at St Andrews. It means quite a lot."

—Alistair Tait

at 3.45pm. Rickman explained that while, "it was still very blowy," and the basic wind speeds were comparable to before the delay, there was a measurable drop in the speeds of the gusts to under 35mph. Only one player, Brian Gay in the course of an 83, was penalised for a ball moving after he had addressed it on the 16th green and Rickman said he called the foul on himself.

McIlroy had hoped if it was to be windy that it would at least be dry. Well, it was dry after he teed-off at 1.30pm, but the wind got him. Ironically, he had made three pars before the suspension but then bogeyed four of the next five holes upon resumption. Out in 40, he was not only tumbling down the leaderboard, but his record of never having shot higher than 69 on the Old Course was being blown away.

With players finding it impossible to feel comfortable over the ball, whether a long shot or a putt, the pace of play slowed to a crawl,

Second Round Scores	
Players Under Par	26
Players At Par	6
Players Over Par	124

Round Two Hole Summary

HOLE	PAR	YARDS	EAGLES	BIRDIES	PARS	BOGEYS	D.BOGEYS	HIGHER	RANK	AVERAGE
1	4	376	0	21	109	26	0	0	13	4.03
2	4	453	0	12	91	46	6	1	4	4.31
3	4	397	0	23	116	17	0	0	15	3.96
4	4	480	0	11	90	50	5	0	5	4.31
5	5	568	4	48	90	11	3	0	17	4.75
6	4	412	0	13	98	40	5	0	9	4.24
7	4	371	0	24	100	31	1	0	12	4.06
8	3	175	0	12	100	42	1	1	10	3.23
9	4	352	0	36	103	15	2	0	16	3.89
OUT	36	3,584	4	200	897	278	23	2		36.79
10	4	386	0	10	110	29	7	0	11	4.21
11	3	174	0	5	89	51	11	0	3	3.44
12	4	348	0	10	98	43	5	0	7	4.28
13	4	465	0	5	79	58	12	2	2	4.53
14	5	618	1	32	101	15	6	1	14	4.98
15	4	455	0	9	99	45	3	0	8	4.27
16	4	423	0	8	99	46	3	0	6	4.28
17	4	495	0	3	77	54	13	9	1	4.67
18	4	357	0	60	88	6	1	1	18	3.69
IN	36	3,721	1	142	840	347	61	13		38.35
TOTAL	72	7,305	5	342	1,737	625	84	15		75.14

It's a Fact

The greatest variation in scores between two successive rounds in The Open was 22 strokes by Robin Davenport in 1966. He recorded 94 in the first round and 72 in the second round. The 17-stroke variation this year by Rory McIlroy, 63 in the first round and 80 in the second round, equalled the seventh greatest variation in Open history.

drawing out the torture to an even greater degree. From leaving the 10th green to arriving at the 12th tee — which is to say playing the par-3 11th — took upwards of 45 minutes. Padraig Harrington had a 77, as did Rose after going out of bounds on the 16th; Geoff Ogilvy had a 78; Ernie Els had a 79; Sir Nick Faldo an 81, and Paul Lawrie an 82; all missed the cut. "The most important thing in the wind is to putt well," said Harrington, "and I didn't putt well." Playing companions John Daly and Andrew Coltart, who had both been in joint third position overnight, had rounds of 76 and 77 respectively to fall off the leaderboard.

McIlroy ended up with an 80. He double-bogeyed the 11th after four-putting and bogeyed the 13th and 15th holes. His 63-80 scores did not represent the largest variation in an Open, but at 17 strokes it was greater than the swing suffered by Rod Pampling who recorded 71-86 at Carnoustie in 1999 and went from the first-round lead to missing the cut. At least McIlroy did not emulate the Australian. In fact, he was still under par, if only just. "I'm here for the weekend so it's not all bad, but definitely a complete contrast to yesterday," he said.

"I have never experienced anything like it before. I felt I played the

Tiger Woods had a 73, his first over-par round on the Old Course since 1995.

After a 63 in the first round, Rory McIlroy tumbled to an 80, tied for 38th place.

Excerpts
FROM THE Press

Robert Allenby was on 144 after no bogeys on Thursday, no birdies on Friday.

Edoardo Molinari's 76 left him on 145.

Toru Taniguchi posted a second 70.

first three holes well and then they called us off the course. From then on I didn't hit it well or put myself in the right places. I was getting very frustrated and, to be honest, I did well to par the last three holes." He did well to front up about it, as well, but then he was headed back to the hotel for "room service, some sleep, and to get ready for tomorrow."

The next morning 30 players were back in position to restart at 6.30am, with Henrik Stenson chipping in for a birdie at the 18th and playing partner Jin Jeong, who qualified by becoming the first South Korean to win the Amateur at Muirfield a month earlier, holing a 10-footer for a 3 to share third place with Casey and Westwood, as well as Spain's Alejandro Canizares, who finished off a 71 that morning. As the only amateur to make the cut, Jeong was assured of the Silver Medal, a remarkable achievement given his first experience of

Phil Mickelson, with a 71, finished as play was suspended.

Camilo Villegas went from 68 to 75.

Padraig Harrington had a 77 to miss the cut.

links golf was the Scottish Stroke Play Champion-ship at Glasgow Gailes just a few weeks earlier.

Darren Clarke, who had three holes left to play, birdied the 18th to post his second successive 70, while Zane Scotland, who first played in The Open at Carnoustie in 1999, also had a 3 at the 18th to celebrate his 28th birthday, which had started slightly earlier than ideally planned with a 4am alarm call. His was the second birthday to be celebrated dur-ing the round — the previous night Thomas Aiken was serenaded by the gallery at the 18th green on his 27th birthday.

Steven Tiley started the second round at six under par and after 10 holes on Friday evening — he did not get to tee-off until 5.30pm — was still on

A 71 put Martin Kaymer on 140.

Vijay Singh bogeyed 16 and 17 for a 73.

His 79 meant Ernie Els had 148, two strokes too many.

With 74, Zach Johnson made the cut on the number.

Stewart Cink posted a 71 for a total of 144.

the same mark. The unheralded professional from Kent had used all his links experience from growing up at Deal's Royal Cinque Ports to battle the high winds. But resuming on the 11th on Saturday morning it all went wrong.

The 27-year-old Challenge Tour player, who tossed and turned in bed for five hours before getting up at 4am, missed the green and three-putted for a double-bogey and three-putted the next. Then he had four bogeys in a row from the 14th. At the 17th it could have been worse since he was up against the wall over the road but escaped with a 5. Now he was in danger of missing the cut but parred the last for a 79. At one over he was inside the cut with a stoke to spare, but he had plummeted from tied for third after his opening 66 to a tie for 56th.

It was not long before Tiley was out again for his third round. It took until after 8.30 on Saturday morning to complete the marathon second round, so the back markers in the third were not off until after 10am. It would be another long day. Meanwhile, Lodewicus Theodorus Oosthuizen, or "Shrek" to his friends and "Daddy" to his tiny baby daughter, could afford to put his feet up.

GONE WITH THE WIND

By Lewine Mair

Paradoxical though this might sound, the wind in Rory McIlroy's sails fizzled out during Friday's 40mph gusts.

Following on from his opening 63, the Ulsterman had started his second round with three straight pars and had bisected the fairway from the fourth tee when the klaxon sounded. Competitors were advised that they could either stay where they were or head to the nearest fleet of mini-buses which were on hand in case there was a need.

McIlroy, Lucas Glover, and Tim Clark made for the buses outside the ropes at the fourth and stayed to await further instructions.

A number of such encampments were dotted round the course, with none more lively than the one to the side of the eighth hole, the hub for all those playing at the far end of the course. While Simon Dyson and Soren Hansen sat down in a sheltered little pocket at the back of the eighth tee, others went straight to the buses which, as luck would have it, were lined up next to a fish-and-chips van. Most started to share platters of chips and experiences.

Thomas Levet was chuckling as he told how, immediately prior to the suspension, he had knocked his approach to a foot at the 10th. He had been revelling in all the applause when suddenly the crowd went quiet. His ball had taken off on a fresh gust on its way to an altogether less praiseworthy destination, some 20 feet from the hole.

Glen Day, at the 11th, had hit a bunker shot to an acceptable five yards. By the time he had exited the bunker, he was looking at a 10-yard putt.

Marcel Siem, as he devoured a hot dog, welcomed South Korea's Jae-Bum Park to the party. "Say," said the bemused German, "this is your first time on a links, isn't it?" Park laughed and answered in the affirma-tive. Having opened with a 76, he was halfway to amassing a second-round 79.

While Ryuichi Oda from Japan enjoyed a cigarette with friends from home, the 2004 Champion, Todd Hamilton, signed autographs and chatted away with the spectators. Hamilton's ball had been oscillating on the green

Impatient to resume play, McIlroy sat on the grass.

on several occasions and, like many another, his overriding concern had been one of having a ball blow away after he had grounded his putter. "If the course had been a tad firmer," he said, "The R&A would have called a halt long before they did."

Three-quarters of an hour after the suspension had started, there was action back at 'Camp Four,' the cluster of vans where McIlroy was based. A Rules official with the Ulsterman's group was hearing that the klaxon would soon be sounding for the resumption of play.

McIlroy, Glover, and Clarke went back to their positions and started on a few bends and stretches. All of which was merely a cue for the gusts to embark on a new burst of energy. McIlroy, for one, sat on the grass.

In the next quieter patch, McIlroy jumped up again, bouncing his ball on the face of his wedge and swinging a couple of clubs together. Once more, he and the rest had to stand down.

Finally, at 3.45pm, they were back in business after a 65-minute delay.

McIlroy's 7-iron, not the most difficult of clubs to which to have to return, did not please him. "It's short and left," confirmed his father, Gerry.

The magic was gone. The young man dropped a shot there and seven more over the round. On Thursday, he had been quizzed on how his record was one of having never once veered into the 70s in the nine rounds he had played over the Old Course. That still applied following his 10th round, an 80.

Afterwards, McIlroy said that his rhythm had been blown. "I've never had an experience like that before," he said. He wondered if the right thing had been done in calling a suspension at all because, in his eyes, the weather at the end of the break was no different than it had been before. A Rules official, John Paramor, explained that while the weather overall did not feel any different, the 40mph gusts had lost some of their steam.

Typically, McIlroy admitted that he deserved most of the blame. "I didn't hit it well and I didn't put myself in the right places to give myself the chance of making any birdies," he said.

Paul Lawrie is a great one for putting things in perspective. When the 1999 Champion was asked about his 82 and to what extent the enforced break had ruined his flow, he very quickly said that he had not been enjoying any flow in the first place. He had indulged in "a jumbo sausage and chips" during the interval. It was an impromptu snack which he cheerfully described as "the highlight of my day."

Third Round

Europeans Trail Dream-Maker

By Andy Farrell

No one expected Louis Oosthuizen to be in first place after 54 holes, and five Europeans were poised to steal his dream.

What does a man do who has a five-stroke lead in The Open Championship but has to wait 29 hours between competitive shots? With the second round being completed on Saturday morning, the cut made and the pairings redrawn for the third round, the leading pair of Louis Oosthuizen and Mark Calcavecchia, two of the earliest finishers on Friday, did not venture onto the Old Course until 4.40pm. "It felt like a week and a half," Oosthuizen said. "I was lying around yesterday, but there is only so much lying around you can do."

Oosthuizen did not get to the golf course until 3pm. He spent the morning watching the Tri Nations rugby match between South Africa and New Zealand. "We got beat badly so it wasn't a good start to the day," he reported. "After that I just relaxed.

Louis Oosthuizen was in full stride after holing a 50-foot birdie putt on the 16th.

It's tough playing that late." Phil Mickelson, who has had his share of late weekend starts in the Majors, although nothing quite this late, called the wait "nerve wracking." And he is used to it. This was only the second time Oosthuizen had played on the weekend of a Major.

Even before he teed-up his five-stroke lead was down to four after Henrik Stenson holed his 5-iron second shot at the 13th for an eagle-2. Then on the first green the South African knocked his birdie putt 10 feet past the hole and missed the one back. Another shot gone, the lead down to three. "It was a slow start," he said. "I was quite a bit nervous on the first. That was a nervous first putt. But I got myself together and made a few par-saves after that."

He needed to. The charge was on. Stenson, guided round by Sir Nick Faldo's old caddie Fanny Sunneson, posted a 67 after a bogey-bogey-birdie finish, but he had started at two under, so his seven-under score in the clubhouse was really no threat to the leader. But Paul Casey certainly was. Casey had played the outward nine brilliantly all week and today was no different. The Englishman birdied the second and the third, then the par-5 fifth to

3

Paul Casey, hitting his approach to the fourth hole, had five birdies on the outward nine and returned a 67 for a total of 205.

Third Round Leaders

HOLE	1	2	3	4	5	6	7	8	9	10	11	12	13	14	15	16	17	18	
PAR	4	4	4	4	5	4	4	3	4	4	3	4	4	5	4	4	4	4	TOTAL
Louis Oosthuizen	[5]	4	4	4	5	4	(3)	3	(3)	4	3	4	4	5	4	(3)	4	(3)	69-201
Paul Casey	4	(3)	(3)	4	(4)	4	(3)	3	(3)	4	3	4	4	5	4	4	4	4	67-205
Martin Kaymer	4	4	(3)	(3)	5	4	4	3	[5]	(3)	3	(3)	[5]	(4)	4	4	4	(3)	68-205
Henrik Stenson	(3)	4	4	4	(4)	4	4	(2)	(3)	4	3	4	(2)	5	4	[5]	[5]	(3)	67-209
Alejandro Canizares	4	4	4	(3)	5	4	4	3	[5]	(3)	3	[5]	4	(4)	4	(3)	[5]	4	71-209
Lee Westwood	4	4	4	[5]	5	[5]	4	3	4	(3)	(2)	4	4	(4)	[5]	4	4	(3)	71-209
Dustin Johnson	4	4	4	4	(4)	4	4	3	4	4	3	(3)	4	5	[5]	4	(3)	(3)	69-210
Nick Watney	4	[5]	(3)	(3)	5	[5]	[5]	3	(3)	4	[4]	4	4	5	(3)	4	4	(3)	71-211
Sean O'Hair	4	4	4	[5]	[6]	4	(3)	3	[5]	4	3	(3)	[5]	(4)	4	4	4	(3)	72-211
Retief Goosen	4	[5]	4	4	5	4	(3)	3	(3)	4	3	4	4	(4)	[5]	4	[6]	(3)	72-211
Ricky Barnes	[5]	4	(3)	4	5	(3)	4	[4]	(3)	[5]	3	4	4	(4)	4	[5]	[5]	(3)	72-211

move from six under to nine under. Now the gap was down to two strokes.

It was windy again. Not as windy as the previous afternoon but a trouser-flapping test nonetheless. Stenson said: "It's really difficult to putt more than anything else."

Casey rolled in a 20-footer on the seventh green, the most exposed part of the course, and suddenly he was only one behind Oosthuizen. The 32-year-old from the twinned parishes of Surrey and Scottsdale, Arizona, was enjoying rediscovering his links touch. After years of going to college in America and adapting his game for the PGA Tour — hit it long, hit it high — it does not come naturally any more, but nothing gave him more satisfaction than a little chip-and-run at the 18th with a 6-iron through the corner of the Valley of Sin to set up a birdie on Thursday. "I had not played a shot like that in years," he said. "I had kind of forgotten how to play those little shots. We used to play links golf all the time. Places like Nairn for the Walker Cup in 1999. I was pretty good at it then, so why not now?"

Casey's only previous top-10 finish in The Open came two years earlier at Birkdale. Despite a few

Martin Kaymer dropped two shots but came in with a 68.

"Every time there is an Open at St Andrews, at least one so-called expert suggests that the venerable Old Course, with its wide fairways, double greens and driveable par 4s, has become an anachronism in the power-hitting world of modern golf."

—**Brian Viner,**
The Independent on Sunday

"Phil Mickelson looks as though he's headed for another Open finish out of the top 10. He had a mini-run derailed with a double-bogey at the 16th and a bogey at the 17th after he had worked his way back to four under for the tournament."

—**Hank Gola,** *New York Daily News*

"Henrik Stenson emerged last night as a shock contender to become the first Swede ever to win The Open. But the most shocked person to see his name climbing up the leaderboard at wind-swept St Andrews was the 34-year-old himself."

—**Graham Otway,** *Sunday Mirror*

"One question. OK. Maybe two. Or three. Or …With one round left in this Open at St Andrews, there seems to be a leaderboard full of them."

—**Melanie Hauser, PGATOUR.com**

"It's already been a rocky year for American golfers, even those not named Tiger Woods. Little that's happened at The Open so far suggests that's about to change."

—**Jim Litke,** *The Associated Press*

Steve Marino's second 69 had him on 214.

Shane Lowry had a 71 to share 12th place.

chances over the years, his best finish in a Major was tied for sixth at the Masters way back in 2004. "That's gone very quickly, I must admit. I desperately want to be a Major Champion. I think I have the ability, I think I'm working hard enough, but that doesn't guarantee anything."

In the pairing behind Casey, Oosthuizen came to the seventh and hit his approach to 10 feet for a birdie to go two ahead again. The same dance played out at the ninth, the driveable par 4. Casey two-putted from 45 feet for a 3 and was out in 31. Oosthuizen hit it on the green and got down in two from 60 feet to be out in 35. Casey had cut his deficit from six to two, but by now Oosthuizen

Stenson: Back on the Radar

At the end of a third-round 67 which left him nicely poised on 209, the 34-year-old Henrik Stenson furnished an expressive summation of that day's weather: "The wind isn't as bad as it was, but it still feels like it's trying to rip your pants off."

Stenson's five-under tally had incorporated good breaks and bad, with the good nothing short of sensational. At the short eighth, for example, he had holed from 60 feet — "a bit of a bomb," to use his own words.

As for his eagle at the 465-yard 13th, that began with a 3-wood which "flew forever," or 320 yards to be precise. His second shot, the only other one involved, was a well-struck lob-wedge from the rough which came down to earth on precisely the intended spot. "And after a while," said Stenson of how he learned of his eagle, "the crowd went crazy."

When it was put to him, "You haven't quite been on our radar in 2010," Stenson laughingly suggested that the interrogator should eschew the euphemisms. "There's no point in being kind," he said. "I've been playing really poorly."

He had tumbled from the Top 10 on the World Ranking to outside the Top 30, "and the way I've played, that's what I've deserved."

At St Andrews, this winner of six European Tour titles was hitting the ball so soundly that the elements were wasting their time trying to tug at anything other than his trousers. Indeed, the only thing being tossed hither and thither was Fanny Sunesson's pony-tail. Stenson has had Sir Nick Faldo's former caddie on the bag for several seasons, with the vastly experienced Sunesson proffering help with the mental side of the game as much as anything else.

Like every other Swede on Tour, Stenson has been on the receiving end of endless cracks as to how the Swedish women are into double figures with their Majors — Annika Sorenstam has 10 on her own — to the men's none.

When asked if he objected to such teasing, Stenson, the owner of a deliciously dry sense of humour, responded that it had been "quite horrible. It's given me sleepless nights." On a more serious note, he suggested that the main failing among his gender was one of not getting into position for the last day.

As he looked at Saturday's unfinished leaderboard, Stenson could see that there was the chance of Louis Oosthuizen staying out of reach. At the same time, however, he made it plain that if the South African were to suffer anything in the way of a mishap, he and his fellow Ryder Cup Swede, Robert Karlsson, could both be in the mix.

—Lewine Mair

Henrik Stenson, who finished on 209, tossed his club after holing his approach shot on the 13th for eagle-2.

Miguel Angel Jimenez ricocheted the ball (circled above) off the stone wall and back onto the 17th green.

After his 73, Tiger Woods blamed his putting.

had got over his nerves and was playing beautifully.

Martin Kaymer was five behind the leader. The German came in with a 68 with just two dropped shots on his card. A three-putt from 100 feet at the 13th might be forgivable, but the birdie chance from six feet at the ninth which turned into a three-putt bogey was his only serious error. He fought back with birdies at the 10th and the 12th and was happy with his four-under effort in the conditions.

As the previous day, the Old Course was giving up good scores only grudgingly. Robert Rock had the day's first 67, helped by holing his second at the seventh for an eagle-2. Ross Fisher had a 68 with five birdies on the inward nine but spoilt it by a double-bogey at the 17th where he went out of bounds with his second shot over the wall behind the road. It was an eventful day at the Road Hole, which was playing harder than on any other day. Miguel Angel Jimenez had quite an adventure. His second finished in a dip in front of the Road Hole

Robert Rock shared the low score with a 67.

Ross Fisher had 68, but double-bogeyed the 17th.

bunker. His attempted lob over the bunker came off too strong and the ball bounced on the road and finished up against the face of the wall.

Part of the thinking behind extending the tee was to bring the road and the wall more into play. Jimenez now recreated a shot thought redundant for the top professionals when he ricocheted the ball into the face and saw it loop back onto the green. The disbelieving face of his playing companion, Peter Hanson, was a picture. Jimenez almost holed the putt for a 5, but the likeable 46-year-old Spaniard, back in top form after victory in Paris, had to settle for a 74 for three under par.

It was the same mark as Rock and Fisher, as well as Camilo Villegas, Lucas Glover, and Tiger Woods. If anyone was going to make a third-round charge, surely it would be Woods, the world number one. But this was not the imperious animal which played such precise golf on the Old Course in 2000 and 2005. He was in a bush at the fifth and that cost a bogey-6 and he also bogeyed the short eighth, so he was going in the wrong direction. He got it back to level for

Low Scores	
Low First Nine	
Paul Casey	31
Robert Rock	31
Low Second Nine	
Martin Kaymer	33
Lee Westwood	33
Ross Fisher	33
Low Round	
Paul Casey	67
Henrik Stenson	67
Robert Rock	67

A 69 got Luke Donald up to a share of 26th place.

Charl Schwartzel was another in-form South African with a 68.

the day, despite back-to-back three-putts at the 13th, for bogey, and the 14th, for par, but then dropped a shot at the 17th. It added up to a second successive 73 and a deficit on the leader of double digits. "I was grinding," he said, "I was as patient as I possibly could be. I was just trying to plod my way along but just didn't get anything going. A total of 35 putts for the round will do that to you."

Nor was Mickelson going anywhere fast, a 70 taking him to two under. US Open champion Graeme McDowell ended up at one under after a 76. Unlike Woods in 2000, there would be no Pebble Beach-St Andrews double. At least his compatriot Rory McIlroy was heading back in the right direction. After a 69, the 21-year-old could still say he had not scored in the 70s on the Old Course. If he was not quite his usual jaunty self, it was very definitely a fine effort to put the

80 of Friday behind him. But for a double-bogey at the 17th, where he caught a gust of wind and ended up by the wall behind the road, it might have been even better.

"I felt I responded quite well to the way everything happened yesterday," McIlroy said. "I'm not going to let one round of golf get me down. Playing in such a strong wind yesterday made today feel not as bad, even if it was still quite strong. I definitely hit a few shots out there that I wasn't able to play yesterday. I think it might be because I had 80 shots yesterday, so I had a little bit of practice."

Someone else feeling a little bit happier was Sergio Garcia, who after a 70 to follow two 71s was on the same four-under score as McIlroy and leading amateur Jin Jeong. Garcia, whose form had deteriorated so badly that he entered The Open with the distinct possibility of missing the Ryder Cup in the autumn, admitted he had been down in the dumps for ages. But he enjoyed his friend Rafael Nadal winning Wimbledon and Spain's footballers winning the World Cup, and on Friday evening in St Andrews had an honest heart-to-heart with family and close friends.

Three Americans, Nick Watney, Sean O'Hair, and Ricky Barnes, were at five under along with Retief Goosen, while Dustin Johnson, one of the biggest hitters in the game, was one better at six under after a 69. Birdies at the final two holes were a nice way to finish for the 26-year-old American, who was not only trying to adapt to the game along the ground but also put behind him the nightmare of Pebble Beach. The 54-hole leader, Johnson crashed to an 82 in the final round. "It is nice to be back in the hunt," he said. "Pebble was one of those funny days in golf, we all have them, but I've tried to learn from things and put it behind me."

Johnson ended the day in seventh place behind a top six of European Tour players. If it was the Alfred Dunhill Links, you could imagine Oosthuizen running away with it. But in The Open anything

Dustin Johnson had a 69 and was seventh alone.

Nick Watney reached the top 10 with his 71.

Round of the **Day**

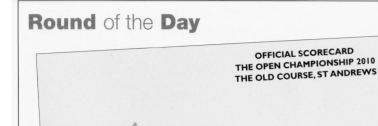

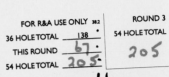

OFFICIAL SCORECARD
THE OPEN CHAMPIONSHIP 2010
THE OLD COURSE, ST ANDREWS

FOR R&A USE ONLY	38.2	ROUND 3
36 HOLE TOTAL	138	54 HOLE TOTAL
THIS ROUND	67	205
54 HOLE TOTAL	205	

Paul CASEY
Game 38
Saturday 17 July at 4:30pm

VERIFIED

ROUND 3

Hole	1	2	3	4	5	6	7	8	9	Out
Yards	376	453	397	480	568	412	371	175	352	3584
Par	4	4	4	4	5	4	4	3	4	36
Score	4	3	3	4	4	4	3	3	3	31

Hole	10	11	12	13	14	15	16	17	18	In	Total
Yards	386	174	348	465	618	455	423	495	357	3721	7305
Par	4	3	4	4	5	4	4	4	4	36	72
Score	4	3	4	4	5	4	4	4	4	36	67

Signature of Marker

Signature of Competitor
Paul Casey

Paul Casey did in nine holes all that was needed for him to post a 67 and join Henrik Stenson and Robert Rock on the low score of the third day. Further, with earlier rounds of 67 and 69, Casey was alone in second place at 205, four strokes behind Louis Oosthuizen.

"I would love to replicate that tomorrow," Casey said. "I'm not sure it would be enough with the way Louis is playing, but I was very happy with that. It was a tough outward nine with the wind. I watched a lot of the golf this morning, and I saw mixed things. I saw some guys making birdies. I saw some guys struggling a bit, so I really didn't know how it was going to go."

But Casey scored five birdies and no bogeys for 31 on the first nine, gaining strokes on the second, third, fifth, seventh, and ninth holes.

"I drove the ball beautifully, and that gave me the opportunity to hit nice iron shots to try and keep it by the hole or into-the-wind putts, and I did that, and I made a lot of birdies," Casey said. "I thought we could do the same coming back home with the wind. We got to about 13, and the wind was certainly a lot less than earlier on. I thought that was a huge break, but I didn't take advantage of it.

"It's a bit disappointing, but all in all, a 67. I mean, I'm very happy with that."

JB Holmes posted his second 70.

Sergio Garcia, 70, was inspired by Spain's football success.

Ricky Barnes hit into the burn and bogeyed the first hole.

could still happen. How many of the contenders stacked up behind him would have a chance the following day depended on how far the South African could forge ahead on the inward nine.

Since that three-putt at the first, Oosthuizen had settled into a relaxed stride. Whenever he needed to secure a par with a decent putt, in it went. Used to playing in the wind at home in Mossel Bay, he was keeping control of the ball impressively. Not a tall man at 5ft 10in, he possesses an effortless power with a well-nurtured and compact swing. Mentally, he was not getting distracted or frustrated, partly thanks to his new routine of looking at a red dot on his glove to begin his pre-shot routine and leave other thoughts alone until the next break in play.

What was also impressive was the way Oosthuizen sailed on despite the tribulations of his playing companion. Calcavecchia did not have the best start, bogeying the first three holes, but it got worse at the long fifth. The American, who had joined the Champions Tour only the previous month, drove into a bunker and had to escape sideways. He then hit a driver off the deck, but the ball veered off to the right into a gorse bush. He played a provisional, but on hearing that a ball had been found in the bush, Calcavecchia picked up his provisional.

Paul Casey (above) had 31 on the outward nine and finished with 67, having all pars coming in.

Mark Calcavecchia and wife Brenda came in with a 77.

Unfortunately, it turned out the ball that had been found was not his, nor was it located within the permitted five minutes.

Not only had he lost a ball, but he had picked up the ball in play (his provisional), which meant a further stroke penalty. Under instruction from the referee, he had to drop a ball where he estimated the provisional had finished, played onto the green and two-putted for a 9. Calcavecchia managed three birdies in a row on the last nine, from the 12th, but ended up with a 77 which saw him tumble down the leaderboard to two under par.

Ahead of Oosthuizen and Calcavecchia, a pair of Englishmen seemed to be carrying the burden of Britain's sporting summer, which so far had yielded little to cheer. While Casey got exactly the start he wanted, Westwood had suffered a couple of three-putts in an outward 38. A long putt on the 10th for his first birdie of the day got the gallery

Paul Casey
Where He Wants to Be

Paul Casey has always said that his best chance to win a Major Championship would come at Augusta and the Major Championship he wanted to win most was The Open. Actually, though, Casey has become such a solid performer now that he could challenge anywhere, on an inland course such as Redstone in Texas where he had won the 2009 Shell Houston Open, on a desert course such as the Ritz-Carlton in Marana, Arizona, where he was beaten in the final of the 2010 Accenture Match Play Championship by Ian Poulter, and now on the links of the Old Course.

By the time Saturday evening came around Casey was doing just that. Only one man was ahead of him. Having started with two 69s, he had a 67 in the third round, one more than his best at St Andrews, to move to within four strokes of Louis Oosthuizen, the leader.

When he is on song Casey is quite something to watch. He walks quickly, rarely spends long over the ball, and those beefy forearms of his enable him to generate considerable clubhead speed which translates into his ball going a long way. He is thoughtful and courteous and can be disarming. He was all these and more in and after his round on Saturday. "I'm not sure whether it was the most controlled round I've ever played in a Major Championship, but it was the most controlled round I have played at St Andrews," he said.

Rounds at St Andrews sometimes resemble games of chess, the positioning of a ball being more important than the distance it has travelled. Casey had done exactly what he should have done, which was to take advantage of the outward nine holes, where he picked up five birdies, and hold on in the wind coming home and not make a mistake. If he had a regret it was that when the wind

started to drop, as it did on the 13th, he wasn't able to take advantage of it as he would have liked.

Casey can be a magnificent driver, sending the ball high and far, and for the first nine he certainly was. He had changed his driver after the first round to one with one half of a degree more loft to help him put more spin on his ball, and this enabled him to drive even better than ever. Get in the right place from the tee to attack St Andrews and a low score can be made, and that is what Casey did. His longest putt was from 20 feet on the seventh hole.

It left him the leading home contender and paired with Oosthuizen for the final round. Just where he wanted to be, in other words. He was only a few weeks away from his 33rd birthday. Was he going to celebrate it as Open Champion?

—John Hopkins

---

in the grandstands out on the loop excited. Then he hit a 5-iron to 15 feet at the 11th and holed that. "If I could have gone out in a couple under I would have felt more in the tournament," Westwood said. "But I've not had any momentum because I've not putted well enough."

Casey was hoping those two putts would spark something for him. "I enjoyed those two birdies because I thought we might feed off each other and make a lot more birdies on the back," Casey said. "But it didn't happen. I haven't really done a thing on the back nine all week."

Westwood had a birdie-bogey exchange at the 14th and 15th holes, then got a 3 at the last after two-putting from 40 feet. A 71 put him at seven under, alongside Stenson and young Spaniard Alejandro Canizares. The son of former Ryder Cup player Jose Maria Canizares, he was enjoying the week of his career to date in his first Open and returned rounds of 67, 71, and 71. "I've won from eight behind before, once at the European Open, but strange things have been happening this week," Westwood said. "It can be done, we know

Third Round Scores	
Players Under Par	**40**
Players At Par	**11**
Players Over Par	**26**

"Defending champ Stewart Cink finished with a quite sensational eagle-2 at the 18th to return a one-under-par 71. Unfortunately, any remote chance the American had of winning back-to-back Opens virtually disappeared long before his glory finish."

—**Ron Scott,** *The Sunday Post*

"You could get a pretty decent score out of Mark Calcavecchia and Louis Oosthuizen on a Scrabble board, and they managed to come up with some funny old numbers in St Andrews as well."

—**Alasdair Reid,** *Sunday Herald*

"It remained a battle for survival, and some were unable to cope. The overnight leader, Louis Oosthuizen, was not among them, however, dropping a shot at the first only to get it back at the sixth."

—**Mike Selvy,** *The Observer*

"Ladies first and now for the men. If women's golf has become accustomed to the prowess of Koreans, then it seems we had better get used to also seeing their names at the top of leaderboards at the male Majors in the years to come. Jin Jeong's comfortable win in the Amateur Championship at Muirfield last month followed wins for Byeong-Hun An in the US Amateur and Han Chang-Won in the Asian Amateur."

—**Douglas Alexander,**
The Sunday Times

In with a 72, Retief Goosen took 6 on the Road Hole.

Robert Karlsson had a 72 after an outward 33.

that. But it depends on the weather, and Louis and Paul seem to be playing well. It will be tough and I'll have to play some good stuff tomorrow." One problem for Westwood was that the late finish meant he could only ice his injured calf once before going to bed.

For Casey there was only frustration. By now it was getting late in the evening, the shadows were lengthening and the wind, finally, dying down. "It almost died when we were on the 13th," Casey said. "I thought that was a huge break, but I didn't take advantage of it." His birdie try at the 13th lipped out and he missed a short putt for a 4 at the 14th. He had parred his way to the 18th where a 3 was almost regulation, but after chipping to four feet he missed a vital chance to cut his overnight deficit.

Round Three Hole Summary

HOLE	PAR	YARDS	EAGLES	BIRDIES	PARS	BOGEYS	D.BOGEYS	HIGHER	RANK	AVERAGE
1	4	376	0	6	60	10	1	0	6	4.08
2	4	453	0	7	52	17	1	0	5	4.16
3	4	397	0	14	59	3	1	0	13	3.88
4	4	480	0	7	50	19	1	0	4	4.18
5	5	568	5	21	43	5	2	1	15	4.77
6	4	412	0	11	53	11	2	0	9	4.05
7	4	371	1	21	46	7	2	0	14	3.84
8	3	175	0	6	62	8	1	0	10	3.05
9	4	352	0	30	42	5	0	0	17	3.68
OUT	**36**	**3,584**	**6**	**123**	**467**	**85**	**11**	**1**		**35.69**
10	4	386	0	10	54	12	1	0	11	4.05
11	3	174	0	5	62	9	1	0	7	3.08
12	4	348	0	14	51	12	0	0	12	3.97
13	4	465	1	2	49	24	1	0	2	4.29
14	5	618	0	28	40	8	1	0	16	4.77
15	4	455	0	9	53	15	0	0	8	4.08
16	4	423	0	7	47	22	1	0	3	4.22
17	4	495	0	5	27	31	12	2	1	4.73
18	4	357	1	46	29	0	1	0	18	3.40
IN	**36**	**3,721**	**2**	**126**	**412**	**133**	**18**	**2**		**36.58**
TOTAL	**72**	**7,305**	**8**	**249**	**879**	**218**	**29**	**3**		**72.27**

The disappointment was compounded because Oosthuizen did exactly what Casey had been trying to do. Apart from keeping any dropped shots off his card — he might have been in trouble at the 17th but his low, punched approach ran to the left edge of the green by the 18th tee and he was able to two-putt from there — he had the bonus of holing a 50-footer over a ridge at the 16th.

Then he hit a superb drive at the last which not only brought the applause of the gallery but the admiration of the diners in the marquee overlooking the first tee and the 18th green. The diners had to press on since it was now past 9pm, but everyone else was watching Oosthuizen intently as he faced a makeable eagle putt from 20 feet. Had he made it, the young leader would have gone to bed with a five-stroke lead. He missed, but tapped in for a 3, and even so had a mighty four-stroke advantage at 15 under par. The final

His 71 put Lee Westwood in a tie for fourth on 209.

Graeme McDowell had 76 and was 14 shots behind.

Sean O'Hair posted his second level-par 72.

Jin Jeong's 74 dropped him out of the top 10.

three-quarters of an hour of another long day, when Oosthuizen had doubled his lead, might just have been crucial to the following day's result.

"I was very happy with the way I handled myself out there and kept my emotions in check," Oosthuizen said. "After the first hole I knew you could so easily just lose it. But I kept really positive and I knew there would be some birdies out there. I spoke to Charl Schwartzel this morning when he finished and he said the pins were a bit more friendly. It took awhile, but I felt I settled in nicely. You know, I don't think anyone thought I was going to be up there. No one can actually say my surname, so they don't even know who I am out there. But it's great being up there and it's great fun."

Both Oosthuizen and Casey had returned three rounds in the 60s. Oosthuizen added a 69 to his earlier 65 and 67. Casey, after two 69s, had scored a 67, a tremendous effort but one that had only trimmed the South African's lead by one. A year ago Casey had suffered a rib injury at The Open of which he only now felt he was completely clear. "Occasionally, even now I feel the muscles in the rib, but in

Tom Lehman returned a 75 to be tied for 26th place.

no way does that affect my golf," he said. "But it's a small reminder that you take a lot of things for granted. Nothing is better than an Open Championship at the Home of Golf, so I'm loving it. I'm loving the fact I'm playing absolutely great golf and I'm four shots behind Louis."

Casey, so prone to throwing in a rogue double or triple-bogey, was the only player in the field not to drop any shots to par in the third round. According to a golf website that provides statistical analysis of how the weather affected each player and the relative scoring averages for every tee time, Casey's 67 came out as the best round of the week, just ahead of McIlroy's opening 63. Despite the imbalance in his round — for the week he was 12 under for the outward nine and one over for the inward half — Casey had probably never played better in a Major Championship, although a 66 at Oakmont in the 2007 US Open might have pipped it.

Inevitably, Casey was reminded that Sir Nick Faldo was the last Englishman to win The Open, at Muirfield in 1987 and 1992, and at St Andrews in 1990. "It would be the ultimate for me," he said. "Probably because links golf is something I've struggled with. I've always thought my best opportunity would be somewhere like Augusta with my ball flight. But I've worked very hard to give myself the opportunity to compete in an Open Championship as I have now. As for Sir Nick's achievements, if I can emulate just a fraction of what

In the Words of the Competitors...

"I was ready to have a little extra going on this week but fully prepared to enjoy it. It's pretty rare that you get to be the defending Champion right here at St Andrews, so I really wanted to enjoy it."

—Stewart Cink

"The greens are the easy part. It's getting to the greens that is the hard part."

—Robert Allenby

"I'm disappointed in myself because I let a good round slide. I had a good opportunity to get back in the tournament and I let it go."

—Phil Mickelson

"I striped it all day. I just didn't get anything out of the round. I'm driving it beautifully and I'm not making any putts."

—Tiger Woods

"It has been a remarkable two tournaments for me in Scotland, winning the Amateur Championship and also to be the only amateur to make the cut here at St Andrews."

—Jin Jeong

"It's a lot of fun. It's new for me, my first Major. It's everything, you know."

—Alejandro Canizares

Playing from the new tee on the Road Hole, young Alejandro Canizares had a par and three bogeys for the week.

Tim Clark made a par from the Road Hole bunker.

Rory McIlroy, against the stone wall, had a double-bogey.

he's achieved ... I remember the bump-and-run he holed at the 18th (in the first round in 1990). I remember watching it. I was probably running out onto the practice ground to work on everything I was watching. But he's certainly a hero of mine and I would love to replicate what he did here."

Oosthuizen remembered another Open, this time at Muirfield in 2002 when his mentor Ernie Els was the Champion. "Ernie gave me a ring this morning saying just to have fun and enjoy it," Oosthuizen said. "I was watching at home when Ernie won and it was something special. And at the end of the year, we had the Ernie Els Invitational at Fancourt and they were showing the highlights on a big screen. We were getting goose bumps seeing it again, but you're always thinking, 'I hope that happens to me.' That's why tomorrow I'm just going to enjoy the moment and have a lot of fun."

THE HARDEST HOLE IN GOLF

By Art Spander

The warnings attached themselves to the memories, and suddenly it was not a golf hole that you were to confront but a terror lying in the weeds. A bit of architecture made human by the weavers of a thousand tales.

You pictured the 17th at St Andrews holding a knife in its teeth and a triple-bogey in its fist. You imagined it must have been the 17th, the Road Hole, about which Dante advised: "Abandon hope, all ye who enter."

The "hardest hole in golf." Ask anyone. Jack Nicklaus. Tom Watson. Most of all Tommy Nakajima, Michael Campbell, and David Duval. The hardest hole in golf. That was before The Open of 2010, when it was made even harder. When it was extended some 40 yards, extended so far the tee had to be placed on an unused course, out of bounds.

"If you designed that hole now," Colin Montgomerie said in his best Colin Montgomerie-ish candour, "you'd be shot. If you said, 'Now, I'm going to put a tee over an old railway on a practice ground and get you to hit over a hotel,' people would think you were off your head."

But the hole was designed, or more accurately created, centuries ago. When the Old Course went clockwise from holes one to 18, not as for the past many decades, counter-clockwise. When it was the second hole, not the 17th. When the concept of par did not exist, and when the debate raged whether it is a par 5 or a par 4.

It's a par 5, says Phil Mickelson, or rather a par 4.8, but on the card it's listed as a 4, since fractions are not part of scoring.

For 109 years, the Road Hole played at around 455 yards. Although, since you were required originally to hit over coal sheds when the railroad spur ran from Leuchars to St Andrews and then over wooden replicas of the sheds, distance was not as important as direction.

But when golfers, with modern equipment, needed only 7-irons or 8-irons, or even 9-irons, for the second shot instead of

5 or 6-irons, The R&A determined a change was required, moving the tee back. Hold your ears, children. Oh, the language.

It was as if someone had turned Buckingham Palace into a fish-and-chips shop.

A British journalist called it "an act of vandalism." Andrew Coltart, a Scot, argued: "When Usain Bolt keeps breaking the 100-metre world record they don't keep sticking another couple of yards on his line to level it up."

On the other side of this debate is Tom Watson, a five-time Open Champion who would, after his wonderful play in 2009 at Turnberry, aged 59, losing in a playoff to Stewart Cink, miss the cut this time. But before that not missing a chance to add some logic.

"They had to add some length to the golf course," Watson said. "I think it was necessary the length the ball goes today."

The green at the 17th is particularly narrow. Immediately to the left is the infamous Road Hole bunker, some five feet deep, from which extrication can be agony. Immediately to the right is a steep bank, of some three feet, which drops to the eponymous road and beyond that a stone wall.

Tommy Nakajima was on the green in two in 1978, putted into the Road Hole bunker,

took four to get out, and two-putted for a 9. When he was asked if he lost concentration, Nakajima responded: "No, I lose count." Jokesters listed the incident as "The Sands of Nakajima."

In 1995, Michael Campbell of New Zealand ruined any chances of victory when he needed three shots to get out. Five years later, David Duval, in the chase the final day, took four swings from the sand and a quadruple-bogey-8.

In 2010, the disasters were minimal, although Sandy Lyle hit his drive onto the roof of the Old Course Hotel and Rory McIlroy's third-round rally was squelched when he double-bogeyed the hole.

The most imaginative and audacious shot of The Open took place at 17 in the third round. From the left of the green, the relentless Miguel Angel Jimenez tried a pitch which bounded over the putting surface and onto a narrow strip of turf between the wall and the dirt road.

Unable to take backswing of any length, Jimenez instead turned around, smacked the ball into the wall, and watched it ricochet onto the green. That he two-putted for a double-bogey didn't matter. Nor was it consequential the trick had been done in 1995 by Jarmo Sandelin, the Swede.

The hole played virtually the same in 2010, with an average of 4.66 strokes, as it did five years earlier, when the average was 4.65. Of the top 10 finishers in 2010, only Nick Watney played the hole at level par. Champion Louis Oosthuizen was two over par.

There were a total of 16 birdies, one on a 130-foot putt in the final round by Rickie Fowler, 173 bogeys, 54 double-bogeys, and 14 "others," meaning "Please don't ask."

Peter Dawson, The R&A's Chief Executive, said the organisation was particularly satisfied with the change to the hole. "I think the 17th tee has been a great success," he remarked. "I said at the beginning of the week we were hoping the road might come more back into play, and by gosh it did."

Can You Say Oosthuizen?

By Andy Farrell

It is pronounced "WHUST-hy-zen" — and all will know it, because the South African is the Champion Golfer of the Year.

For a first-time winner of one of the game's most cherished prizes, Louis Oosthuizen won the 150th Anniversary Open Championship like a multiple Major Champion. The 27-year-old South African's seven-stroke victory was that commanding.

It could have been Sir Nick Faldo from 1990, when he came home five clear of the field, or Tiger Woods in 2000 or 2005, when the world number one won by eight and five strokes respectively. They both enjoyed the same exultant march up the 18th hole of the Old Course knowing victory was at hand, just as Oosthuizen did this time. Add Jack Nicklaus, Seve Ballesteros, and John Daly to the roll of honour and you have to go back nearly half a century to Tony Lema in 1964, following Kel Nagle at the Centenary Open of 1960, to find a St

Andrews Champion who had not previously won an Open or any of the other Major Championships.

Here was a new Champion Golfer of the Year who in four, short days had become a seasoned winner before our very eyes. He became the sixth South African to win a Major Championship, joining Retief Goosen and Trevor Immelman, as well as the three other Open Champions: Bobby Locke, Gary Player, and Ernie Els. Not bad for a golfer whose nickname was borrowed from a lovable ogre.

"The Shrek is on the move," said Goosen even before Oosthuizen had reached the 18th and completed his epic journey. "It's nice to see. I knew he had a lot of talent. The guy's got one of the best swings on Tour. I think he'll be around for many years to come."

Rory McIlroy, who beat Oosthuizen at the 2009 Dubai Desert Classic but finished eight adrift here, said: "We've all known Louis has been a great player for a long time. He hits it great, is technically very sound, and does everything very well. He needed that win early this season on the European Tour to give him the confidence to challenge for the biggest events. He and his wife have a new baby now, so

A smiling Louis Oosthuizen became the fourth South African to win The Open Championship.

Henrik Stenson couldn't challenge with one birdie, 17 pars.

For Rory McIlroy it was an opportunity missed after a 280.

Lee Westwood was second alone on 279, finishing with 70.

he's in a pretty good place at the moment."

Lee Westwood, who finished as the distant runner-up, said: "He is very impressive. He flights the ball very well when it gets windy. I can see why he's doing well this week. He has good penetration on his iron shots and obviously has a lot of bottle. This is the first time he has contended at a Major Championship and he's tackled everything that's been thrown at him like an old pro."

Paul Casey, who played alongside Oosthuizen in the final pairing of the final round, immediately congratulated the new Champion as they shook hands on the 18th green. "I just told him what I thought of that performance," Casey said. "That was four days of tremendous golf. He didn't flinch today. His rhythm looked superb, he drove the ball beautifully, he was very calm. I've played with him many a time, but that was a world-class performance."

Fourth Round Leaders

HOLE	1	2	3	4	5	6	7	8	9	10	11	12	13	14	15	16	17	18	
PAR	4	4	4	4	5	4	4	3	4	4	3	4	4	5	4	4	4	4	TOTAL
Louis Oosthuizen	4	4	4	4	5	4	4	[4]	(2)	4	3	(3)	4	5	4	4	[5]	4	71-272
Lee Westwood	4	4	4	4	5	4	4	3	(3)	4	3	[5]	(3)	(4)	4	4	[5]	(3)	70-279
Rory McIlroy	4	4	4	4	(4)	4	4	3	(3)	4	[4]	(3)	4	(4)	4	4	4	(3)	68-280
Henrik Stenson	4	4	4	4	5	4	(3)	3	4	4	3	4	4	5	4	4	4	4	71-280
Paul Casey	4	[5]	4	4	5	(3)	4	3	(3)	4	3	[7]	4	5	[5]	4	4	4	75-280
Retief Goosen	4	4	4	4	(4)	4	4	3	4	4	3	4	4	5	4	4	4	(3)	70-281
Robert Rock	4	4	4	4	(4)	(3)	4	[4]	(3)	4	[4]	4	4	(4)	4	4	4	(3)	69-282
Sean O'Hair	4	4	4	4	5	(3)	4	3	4	(3)	3	4	[6]	(4)	4	4	[5]	(3)	71-282
Nick Watney	4	4	4	[5]	[6]	4	4	3	(3)	(3)	3	[5]	(3)	5	4	4	4	(3)	71-282
Martin Kaymer	[5]	4	4	4	5	(3)	4	(2)	4	[5]	3	[5]	4	(4)	(3)	[5]	[5]	[5]	74-282

Peter Dawson, the Chief Executive of The R&A and the man who had to get his tongue around the Afrikaner vowels of the Champion Golfer's surname at the presentation ceremony, said: "Based on the margin of victory, his demeanour on the golf course, the quality of his game, and the steady progress he's been making on the World Ranking and Tour events, I think we can mark him very much as a player on the rise. Every great Open Champion has to win for the first time somewhere, that's self-evident. But I, for one, would not be surprised to see him win again."

Oosthuizen started the year at 89th in the World Ranking, won his first European Tour event at the Open de Andalucia in March and, despite missing the cut at the Masters and the US Open, was ranked 54th in the world on arrival at St Andrews. On departure, he was up to 15th. He also left with the Gold Medal, a replica of the original Challenge Belt, presented by the captain of Prestwick, Brian Morrison — "It's a little too big for me" — and, of course, the Claret Jug, which he refused to let go of, whether celebrating into the night at the Jigger Inn or for a few short hours in bed, once he was handed it by The Royal and Ancient Golf Club's Captain Colin Brown.

"To win an Open Championship is special," Oost-

A 7 on the 12th dropped Paul Casey to a share of third place.

Teeing off here on the par-4 sixth, Casey got the first of his two birdies but was four over on the inward nine.

Alvaro Quiros posted 67 to equal the low round of the day.

huizen said, "but to win it here at St Andrews, it's something you dream about." For South Africans everywhere there was something else that made the day even more special and Oosthuizen began his victory speech by wishing Nelson Mandela a happy 92nd birthday. "I didn't realise until this morning when I was looking at the news on the internet," he said. "But I thought of him as I was walking up the 18th fairway. What he has done for our country is unbelievable."

Oosthuizen also paid tribute to all those who had helped him during his career, especially his family and his mentor, Els. He was now the first graduate of the Ernie Els Foundation at Fancourt to win a Major Championship. Els thought it was fitting that the new Champion had already started a foundation for children at his home club of Mossel Bay.

Retief Goosen, on 70 for sixth place at 281, gave South Africa another top-10 player.

"Louis Oosthuizen walked over the Swilcan Bridge toward a victory that was never in doubt at St Andrews, another big moment in sports for South Africa. This celebration, though, carried a different tune. The drone of vuvuzelas, the rage at the World Cup, was replaced by the skirls of bagpipes coming from behind The Royal and Ancient Clubhouse. For the 27-year-old South African, the sound could not have been sweeter."

—**Doug Ferguson,**
The Associated Press

"Throughout a march toward The Open Championship that went from improbable to inexorable with each stride down the Old Course's hardening fairways Sunday, three things about Louis Oosthuizen did not change: his demeanour, his swing tempo, and his resilience."

—**Larry Dorman,**
The New York Times

"It was the stuff of dreams. Rory McIlroy removed his cap and waved to the galleries as he made his way over the Swilcan Bridge to take on the 12-foot putt that stood between him and an eagle at the last. He could not enjoy it, though. By his own admission, McIlroy was still thinking about Friday and what might have been."

—**Matthew Dunn,** *Daily Express*

"It would be difficult to find anybody in the world who is more proud of Louis right now," Els said. "He is a wonderful kid. You cannot find a better one and I am so pleased for him.

"I thought long before anybody had heard of him that he was going to be an exceptional player. What I saw in him as a youngster was that he had a lot of natural ability plus he has the length and gets the ball out there, which are important factors in the modern game. Louis is now The Open Champion. His life will change. He won't."

But to get to where he was now, he had changed already, watching and learning from Els and the rest. "It was just a matter of grow-

Jeff Overton, with his second 69, tied for 11th place.

Trevor Immelman posted 68 in both the first and last rounds.

Robert Rock shared seventh place despite 78 on Friday.

ing up, really," Oosthuizen said. "Any youngster makes mistakes on the golf course and it frustrates you. If you look at the older guys on tour who have all that experience, when they make a bogey or a double-bogey, they just go on to the next hole. I thought to myself, the quicker I can get around that, the quicker I'm going to win tournaments."

With daughter Jana being born at the start of the year, having his own family also played its part. "My wife and child have a lot to do with it, relaxing me and not just thinking about golf. They have got me settled even better," he said.

Oosthuizen's wife, Nel-Mare, had to wipe away tears at the presentation. "We'll remember this day for the rest of our lives," she said. "I said to Louis at the start of the week that I needed a new vase — we can use the Claret Jug now!" But given that Louis thought it too special to drink from, at least now that Turnberry Champion Stewart Cink had cleaned up the barbeque sauce, flowers may not be going in there, either.

Nel-Mare said of her husband that morning:

Round Four Hole Summary

HOLE	PAR	YARDS	EAGLES	BIRDIES	PARS	BOGEYS	D.BOGEYS	HIGHER	RANK	AVERAGE
1	4	376	0	16	55	6	0	0	15	3.87
2	4	453	0	9	60	6	2	0	9	4.01
3	4	397	0	13	57	7	0	0	13	3.92
4	4	480	0	3	53	18	3	0	3	4.27
5	5	568	0	26	45	3	3	0	16	4.78
6	4	412	0	13	57	7	0	0	14	3.92
7	4	371	1	11	58	6	1	0	12	3.94
8	3	175	0	4	64	8	0	1	7	3.09
9	4	352	3	33	39	2	0	0	17	3.52
OUT	**36**	**3,584**	**4**	**128**	**488**	**63**	**9**	**1**		**35.33**
10	4	386	0	14	52	11	0	0	11	3.96
11	3	174	0	3	62	11	1	0	6	3.13
12	4	348	0	8	49	17	2	1	4	4.21
13	4	465	0	7	50	19	1	0	5	4.18
14	5	618	0	21	40	13	3	0	10	4.97
15	4	455	0	6	60	9	2	0	8	4.09
16	4	423	0	1	61	10	2	3	2	4.29
17	4	495	0	3	28	33	13	0	1	4.73
18	4	357	4	37	32	4	0	0	18	3.47
IN	**36**	**3,721**	**4**	**100**	**434**	**127**	**24**	**4**		**37.03**
TOTAL	**72**	**7,305**	**8**	**228**	**922**	**190**	**33**	**5**		**72.35**

"He was all funny and joking so I know he was nervous." Oosthuizen arrived at the course with a four-stroke lead over Casey, but the nerves were calmed by a phone call from Player. "We had a little chat and he was just saying to be calm out there, have a lot of fun and realise the crowd was probably going to be on Paul's side," he said. "But then he told me the story of when he played against Arnold Palmer when he won his first Masters. He said they wanted to throw stuff at him, but he was so focused on winning at Augusta. It meant a lot, him phoning me up."

Player and Els were not the only former Champions on his side. After his warm-up on the practice range, he was being driven to the first tee when the car was stopped and a head popped through a window. "Good luck, kid. I'm rooting for you," said Tom Watson.

Weather conditions were not as severe as the

Matt Kuchar moved up with 71-69 in the last two rounds.

Lee Westwood was runner-up in a Major for the second time.

Robert Karlsson was never over par.

Luke Donald finished with two 69s.

previous three days, but the wind was just beginning to really pick up again as Oosthuizen and Casey arrived on the first tee at 2.05pm. Casey was the first Englishman to be in the final pairing of The Open since Faldo in 1993, when he ended runner-up to Greg Norman. Faldo had said earlier in the week how the pressure in the final round of a Major was "10-fold" that of a regular tournament. With that in mind, Casey needed to get off to the perfect start and he hit his approach over the Swilcan Burn to six feet.

But Casey missed the putt, a vital chance even so early in the day. Worse, he was short at the second and could not get up and down. It was only his third bogey of the week, plus a triple-bogey, but the South African's lead was back up to five strokes. "If I could have put him under some pressure, it could have been different," Casey said.

The Runners-Up
A Week of Promise for European Golf

It was debatable who was happier as the sun set on The Open Championship: South African golf fans or European Ryder Cup captain Colin Montgomerie.

Louis Oosthuizen may have won the Claret Jug with Montgomerie trailing in a tie for 68th, but the boost The Open gave Montgomerie's Ryder Cup hopes was immeasurable.

Six potential European Ryder Cuppers finished behind Oosthuizen in the top 11. Ten potential European team members finished in the top 14. Lee Westwood finished second; Rory McIlroy, Henrik Stenson, and Paul Casey tied for third; Martin Kaymer tied for seventh, while Alvaro Quiros and Luke Donald were just outside the top 10, tied for 11th. Sergio Garcia, Robert Karlsson, and Ignacio Garrido finished tied for 14th.

Take Oosthuizen out of the equation and it's conceivable the European team would have included holders of both the US Open and Open Championship trophies.

For Westwood it was a case of knocking on a Major Championship door for the fifth time and the door not opening. He might have won his first Major if not for Oosthuizen having the week of his life. Westwood finished runner-up in a Major for the second time in three tries, following the Masters. The world number three left St Andrews with four top-three finishes in his last five Majors. At least he finished one spot closer to the Claret Jug than 12 months previously, when he bogeyed the 72nd hole to miss a playoff.

"I keep putting myself into contention in these Major Championships and keep finishing in the top three," Westwood said. "Hopefully one of these chances will turn into a trophy."

Westwood started as one of the favourites. However, like the Masters, when Phil Mickelson denied him the green jacket, he was simply outplayed.

"If you get close and lose, then there's disappointment. But I didn't even get within eight shots," Westwood said. "I played okay all week without really doing anything too special. I didn't make enough opportunities that my long game presented. Didn't putt well enough. My short game wasn't quite sharp enough."

At least Casey got close. He got within three shots of the lead when Oosthuizen bogeyed the eighth. Casey's challenge ended at the 12th when he drove into a gorse bush and made a triple-bogey-7. "I'm going to win a Major. It's just a matter of time," Casey said. "This week just wasn't my week."

Not Casey's week or Westwood's, but a good one for Montgomerie.

"I can pick two teams here that can beat each other on any given day," Montgomerie said. "That's the strength and that's the depth of European golf. In any form of business, and this is one, if standards rise the competition has to follow suit, which is great for me."

—Alistair Tait

Sergio Garcia had a steady week with 71, 71, 70, and 72 for a total of 284.

Low Scores	
Low First Nine	
Matt Kuchar	32
Ian Poulter	32
Low Second Nine	
Luke Donald	32
Rickie Fowler	32
Low Round	
Alvaro Quiros	67
Rickie Fowler	67

Charl Schwartzel finished on 284.

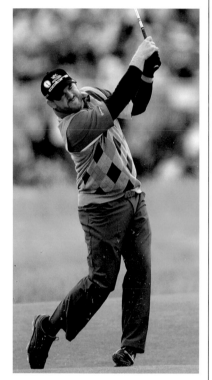

JB Holmes had two 70s, two 72s.

Nick Watney tied for seventh place.

Rickie Fowler started with a 79, then posted 67s twice and tied for 14th place.

Edoardo Molinari scored well to start and finish, but not the two middle rounds.

"But I'm not sure if I had put him under pressure he would have flinched anyway. He didn't miss a shot."

Oosthuizen was hardly in any trouble, except at the par-5 fifth, where he was short left of the green and nearer the 13th pin. But he chipped up and two-putted for his par. Birdies were nonexistent for anyone in the final few groups until Martin Kaymer got a 3 at the sixth. The German missed a chance at the next but got a 2 at the eighth to get to nine under but he could never get to double figures under par. Sweden's Henrik Stenson made a 3 at the seventh, but the rest of his round was made up of 17 pars. Westwood made eight pars until he got a 3 at the ninth.

Chasing the leader already appeared a forlorn task. Colin Montgomerie said that with the final-day hole locations for The Open at St Andrews, you would always want to be the pursued rather than the pursuer. Monty should know, having failed to overtake Woods in 2005. Anyone who thought Oosthuizen might be fazed by front-running needed to look back at the Telkom PGA Championship in 2008 — Oosthuizen won it by 14 strokes, a Sunshine Tour record, at 28 under par.

It was not quite those proportions yet and it was not won yet, either. Not when he bogeyed the short eighth. He was so far away on the green that he elected to chip and then misread the 15-footer for par. Suddenly, Casey was only three back and now he drove the green at the short par-4 ninth.

Round of the **Day**

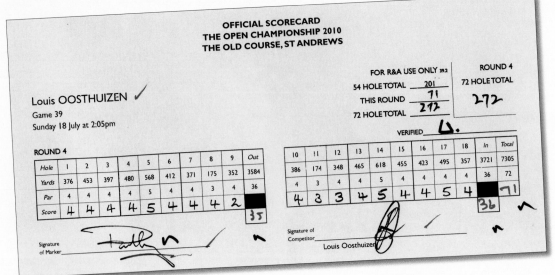

OFFICIAL SCORECARD
THE OPEN CHAMPIONSHIP 2010
THE OLD COURSE, ST ANDREWS

FOR R&A USE ONLY 292

54 HOLE TOTAL	201
THIS ROUND	71
72 HOLE TOTAL	272

ROUND 4
72 HOLE TOTAL
272

Louis OOSTHUIZEN ✓
Game 39
Sunday 18 July at 2:05pm

VERIFIED L.

ROUND 4

Hole	1	2	3	4	5	6	7	8	9	Out
Yards	376	453	397	480	568	412	371	175	352	3584
Par	4	4	4	4	5	4	4	3	4	36
Score	4	4	4	4	5	4	4	4	2	35

Hole	10	11	12	13	14	15	16	17	18	In	Total
Yards	386	174	348	465	618	455	423	495	357	3721	7305
Par	4	3	4	4	5	4	4	4	4	36	72
Score	4	3	3	4	5	4	4	5	4	36	71

Signature
of Marker_____

Signature of
Competitor_____
Louis Oosthuizen

Louis Oosthuizen was playing solidly on the outward nine but without much to show for it, seven straight pars then a bogey on the eighth hole, where he thought he made a good putt but misread it. "I was one over through eight, which I thought should have been one or two under," Oosthuizen said. "I had it in my head that I needed one putt to really get my rhythm going. And that eagle on nine, that got me started."

On the 352-yard, par-4 ninth, Oosthuizen was confident with his driver — "I knew I wasn't going to lose it left, the shot I wanted to hit, and I'm hitting my driver really well" — and he drove the ball onto the green, pin-high, 45 feet from the hole. "I just knew I needed something to go in, any birdie, just to two-putt was very important for me," he said. "After I hit it, it was never anywhere else. It was tracking and went in."

With the eagle-2 on the ninth, Oosthuizen made the turn in one under and was on his way to the 71 that resulted in his seven-stroke victory. He birdied from 14 feet after a chip shot to the 12th hole at the same time that his playing companion, Paul Casey, was taking a triple-bogey.

"I made good putts," Oosthuizen said. "I made good putts when I had to. I rarely missed a putt under six feet this week. … But I think it was a much tighter race until the 12th hole today."

Fourth Round Scores	
Players Under Par	**32**
Players At Par	**10**
Players Over Par	**35**

Photographers had found a new subject.

Oosthuizen rolled in a 45-foot eagle putt at the ninth, and was congratulated by caddie Zack Rasego (below).

Oosthuizen responded magnificently, also finding the putting surface and inside his opponent. Casey putted up for a birdie, but Oosthuizen holed his 45-footer for an eagle and the gentle punch of the air was as good as a victory salute. "I had it in my head that I needed one putt to really get my rhythm going," Oosthuizen said. "And that eagle on nine got me started."

It was better than good. They were both out in 35 so the deficit was back to four. It was Casey's worst return of the week on the outward nine and Oosthuizen had the better record on the inward nine. Elsewhere, the best scores of the day had come from Alvaro Quiros and Rickie Fowler, dressed in all orange, with a pair of 67s, while there were three 68s, among them McIlroy. The first-round leader now had 11 rounds in the 60s to his name on the Old Course and still none in the 70s. Three of his rounds here added up to 16

Tiger Woods tied for 23rd after a change of putters.

under par, which turned out to be the winning score.

Without that ugly 80 in the second round, McIlroy had shown he really was playing well enough to have challenged. But to recover from his personal nightmare with such a spirited weekend to tie for third place showed real resolve. "I couldn't help but think about Friday going up the last hole there," said the 21-year-old Northern Irishman. "If I had just stuck in a little bit more and held it together, it could have been a different story.

"When you start off shooting 63 in any golf tournament you have to fancy your chances. But I hadn't played in a wind like that for

In Search of Tiger

St Andrews was where the domination would be on display once more. Or so we believed. Or so he believed. Tiger Woods and the Old Course, mystery and history, the same old questions from the media, literal and figurative, but presumably a new, definite answer.

The year had been torment and possibility. And contrition and rehabilitation. Now, at the Old Course, where Tiger won The Open in 2000 and 2005, where Tiger said he would choose to play every Major every year, the hope of restoration.

He was the betting favourite. He was the gallery favourite.

He just wasn't the golfer he used to be.

And maybe, having reached the age of 34, might never be again, although this is too early to speculate. Too early to note the window of domination in golf doesn't stay open very long, except in rare cases, except for Gary Player or the man Tiger Woods is chasing, Jack Nicklaus.

Jack has those 18 Majors, the last victory coming when he was 46. It was an aberration. Jack won a US Open in 1962. Jack won a Masters in 1986, a stretch of 24 years. That's rare, very rare.

Tiger won his first Major in 1997 at 21. He won his 14th in 2008, 11 years later at 32. Ben Hogan won all his Majors over seven years, Arnold Palmer his over six years, Tom Watson his over eight years. Watson told Joe Posnanski of the American magazine *Sports Illustrated:* "I had my time. How long can anyone expect to be the best in the whole world?"

Woods, although first in the World Ranking, looked far from being the best in the 2010 Open. He had an encouraging 67 the first day, but after that Woods never had a chance. Every move forward was countered by one to the rear. The fourth round, Tiger began birdie, birdie. The excitement halted with a double-bogey at the fourth.

It was the putting, said Tiger, of the reason he came in tied for 23rd at 285, 13 shots behind the winner, Louis Oosthuizen. It was the putting, the very strength of his game. Until St Andrews 2010.

"I must have three-putted nine or 10 times," said Woods. "You can't expect to win if you're to have nine or 10 three-putts."

Woods came in with the dream of being the first to win at St Andrews three times. He drove the ball well. He hit his approaches well enough. He putted terribly, both with his new Nike and then on Sunday, when he returned to his Scotty Cameron.

Before last winter, 2010 was going to be Tiger's year, three of the Majors played on courses, Augusta, Pebble Beach, and St Andrews, where he had won a combined seven times.

The figure remained unchanged. The mystery remained unsolved. And Tiger is growing older .

—Art Spander

a long time and I didn't deal with it very well. There are a lot of positives, but I'm still a bit disappointed to be honest."

Woods hoped a change of putters back to his trusty old Scotty Cameron would herald a leap up the leaderboard into the top 10, but it was not to be. He tied for 23rd and for the first time at St Andrews since 1995, when as an amateur he did not have his own private jet, the flight home did not include the precious cargo of the Claret Jug.

Another former Champion, Tom Lehman, finished with the shot of the week at the 18th when he drove to two feet for an eagle. Jin Jeong, the Amateur Champion from South Korea via Melbourne, finished in style with a 2 as he collected the Silver Medal as the leading amateur, while Luke Donald finished birdie-eagle to leap up the leaderboard to a tie for 11th. What a finish his brother, Christian, still out on the course caddieing for Casey, would have liked for his employer.

It would not have made any difference. At the short but perilous 12th hole Casey pulled his drive into a gorse bush. The ball was

It's a Fact

Louis Oosthuizen was the fourth player from South Africa to win The Open, following countrymen Bobby Locke, Gary Player, and Ernie Els. South Africa and Australia are now tied with four Open Champions each. There have been 37 Open Champions from Great Britain and Northern Ireland and 27 from the United States. Countries with one Open Champion each are Argentina, France, New Zealand, Republic of Ireland, Spain, and Zimbabwe.

The margin became eight shots at the 12th, when Casey hit into a gorse bush for a triple-bogey-7 while Oosthuizen made birdie.

Championship Totals	
Rounds Under Par	171
Rounds At Par	50
Rounds Over Par	227

found by an eagle-eyed spotter, but Casey had to take an unplayable, had a blind third shot, and came up short of the green. Then it became a comedy of errors. His fourth went over the back of the shelf-like green and he ended up with a triple-bogey-7, his second of the week.

While all that was going on, Oosthuizen calmly birdied the hole, sinking a 14-footer with ruthless efficiency. It was the thing an old Champion would do. It was the final knockout blow. He was now eight shots ahead. "It felt a much tighter race today until the 12th hole," he said. "That was a big change. All of a sudden, it was mine to throw away. Knowing St Andrews, 14 was a dangerous drive and 17 was a dangerous drive. But I'd been hitting my driver so well and I knew I wasn't going to lose it right if I hit it very hard, which I did on those two holes. I'm proud of the way I held my nerve on the back nine."

Strong driving again held Oosthuizen in good stead. His only problem at the long 14th was finding a bunker with his second shot, the first time he had been in sand all week, so he could not quite emulate Tiger from 2000. He took three to get down, but that

Championship Hole Summary

HOLE	PAR	YARDS	EAGLES	BIRDIES	PARS	BOGEYS	D.BOGEYS	HIGHER	RANK	AVERAGE
1	4	376	0	79	328	55	4	0	12	3.97
2	4	453	0	53	291	108	12	2	6	4.18
3	4	397	0	80	347	38	1	0	14	3.91
4	4	480	0	31	304	116	15	0	4	4.25
5	5	568	13	172	243	29	8	1	17	4.68
6	4	412	0	64	317	74	10	1	10	4.07
7	4	371	2	91	310	58	5	0	13	3.94
8	3	175	0	32	347	81	4	2	8	3.14
9	4	352	4	159	275	26	2	0	16	3.71
OUT	**36**	**3,584**	**19**	**761**	**2,762**	**585**	**61**	**6**		**35.85**
10	4	386	0	64	333	58	11	0	11	4.03
11	3	174	0	24	327	102	13	0	5	3.22
12	4	348	1	64	303	89	7	2	9	4.09
13	4	465	1	31	277	137	18	2	2	4.31
14	5	618	1	143	252	58	11	1	15	4.87
15	4	455	0	42	321	98	5	0	7	4.14
16	4	423	0	24	318	110	10	4	3	4.25
17	4	495	0	16	208	174	54	14	1	4.67
18	4	357	6	186	254	16	3	1	18	3.63
IN	**36**	**3,721**	**9**	**594**	**2,593**	**842**	**132**	**24**		**37.22**
TOTAL	**72**	**7,305**	**28**	**1,355**	**5,355**	**1,427**	**193**	**30**		**73.07**

A birdie on the last hole secured second place for Westwood, who posted a 70 for a total of 279.

Excerpts FROM THE Press

Stephen Gallacher was the low Scot.

Dustin Johnson tied for 14th.

Sean O'Hair got a share of seventh.

meant another solid par. The 16th, with its devious pin placement, was parred and then at the 17th he aimed for the front right of the green but tugged it a tad. It was never far enough to reach the bunker, but he had to negotiate around it and took three to do so even though it meant a bogey.

Casey missed the green at the 15th to drop another shot and came home in 40. His 75 meant he has still not broken 70 in the final round of The Open and he needed to today. "I'm disappointed, but even if you take away the mistakes I made, the couple of 7s I've had this week, I don't think it was good enough to get near Louis," Casey said. He finished at eight under in a tie for third place — his best result in a Major Championship — with McIlroy and Stenson, who had a one-birdie 71.

Kaymer had an adventurous inward nine, including bogeys at the last three holes, after visiting the road at the 17th and after four-putting at the last, one into the Valley of Sin, one out and two on the more level bit of the green. A 74 left him tied for seventh place on six under, one behind Goosen.

Westwood, with a 70, two-putted the 18th green for a birdie which

Ignacio Garrido had a steady performance and finished with a 71 to tie for 14th place.

gave him sole possession of second place at nine under. It was his second runner-up finish of the season following his second place at the Masters and his fourth top-three finish in five Majors, going back to Turnberry in 2009 when he had been bitterly disappointed to bogey the last and miss out on the Stewart Cink-Tom Watson playoff.

This time he said: "Whether I won the tournament today was in the hands of other people. Louis obviously played great and thoroughly deserves to win. So there's not even any real disappointment. If you get close and lose, then there's disappointment, but I didn't even get within eight shots today."

Yet here was a man who had capitalised on his very first opportunity to win a Major. Even through the 71st hole, Oosthuizen was wise enough not think anything was certain "until the last putt goes in." But after he drove to the front of the green at the last, "I felt that was it," he said. "I'm definitely not going to 10-putt from there." Leaving the final tee, he patted caddie Zack Rasego on the back and thanked him for his help. He also told him to forget about the talk of splitting up from earlier in the week. For Rasego, it was a victory for a rainbow alliance on behalf of the Rainbow Nation.

The sunglasses came off and the hat, too, as he saluted the gallery

John Daly displayed his colours.

Oosthuizen performed like a multiple Major Champion — even for the photographers.

Jin Jeong displayed the Silver Medal.

Following pages, Oosthuizen smashed a drive on the 18th tee before his walk to glory.

all the way around the 18th hole. St Andrews was offering its usual thunderous ovation for the new Champion. There were no vuvuzelas, they prefer the pipes at the Home of Golf, but Oosthuizen would thank all the South Africans in the gallery, which for the third day running was around 43,000, taking the total for the week of those braving the elements to 201,000. Up at the green, he took three putts to get the job done, a dog barking in the distance as he tried for a birdie, but it was not to be.

A par for a 71 concluded a sequence of scores that were two strokes higher than the day before — 65 (no Champion had ever scored as low on the opening day), 67, 69, and 71 for a total of 272, 16 under par, as he joined Locke from 1957 as a St Andrews Champion. He equalled the seventh largest winning margin in Open history, but only Woods in 2000, when he won by eight, had done better in modern times.

So commanding was this victory, the man from Mossel Bay denied us any chance of any late drama. But that was not his fault, far from it. Just as it was not his fault we could not pronounce his name. We know it now. Louis Oosthuizen — it's on the Claret Jug forever.

TESTIMONY TO HIS CHARACTER

By John Hopkins

As Louis Oosthuizen and Paul Casey began their last round over the Old Course, a man settled down in front of a television at his home in Florida. Normally, Greg Norman might watch golf for a few minutes before turning his hands to other things. On this day though he was transfixed by what was unfolding a few thousand miles to the east and it would be nearly four hours before he would get up again. Later, he would ring Oosthuizen and congratulate him. "Mr Norman told me that he had never watched a round from start to finish before like that. I was flattered," The Open Champion said.

There are signposts here in this anecdote to the sort of person the new Open Champion is. His use of the word Mr suggests an unusual respect for an elder person. The surprise and modesty in his voice as he retells this story indicates a modest manner. And there, in the fact that the play of a little-known South African, aged 27, round the most famous course in the world could cause one of the game's greatest players to remain in his seat for 240 minutes or so, you get a measure of how significant Oosthuizen's performance was. Golf has its one-Major Championship wonders, but there seems to be more reason than usual to think that Oosthuizen will not be one of them. He did not so much win this Open as run away with it, his victory coming by seven strokes.

Oosthuizen became the fourth South African to take ownership for a year of the handsome Claret Jug trophy, the latest in a line of men from that country to triumph in Major Championships. Arthur D'Arcy Robert Locke won The Open in 1949, 1950, 1952, and at St Andrews in 1957. Gary Player won Opens in three decades, 1959, 1968, and 1974, and at Muirfield in 2002 it was Ernie Els' turn to triumph.

Physically, Oosthuizen is 5ft 10in, weighs little more than 12st, and hits the ball with elegance. "He is very easy to watch," Dave McNeilly, the caddie, said one night. "Lovely balance." In contrast, Locke was portly, favoured plus-fours, a white cap, and white shoes, and moved down the fairways "like a stately galleon" according to Pat Ward-

The Oosthuizen family — Louis, baby Jana and Nel-Mare.

Thomas, the golf writer. He hit every shot with a distinct right-to-left flight, even his putts.

Oosthuizen had been 54th in the World Ranking and rated 200-1 to win at the start of the week, which is why he arrived not so much under the radar as off it, a complete outsider. He had only one victory — the Open de Andalucia in March 2010 — since starting to compete on the European Tour in 2003, and he had a dismal record in the eight Major Championships in which he had competed — missing the halfway cut in seven and finishing last in the other.

What do we make of The Open Champion? "Louis comes from a very humble background," said Johann Rupert, the South African-born industrialist who is chairman of that country's PGA. "He is like Lee Trevino and Mr Hogan. He has had to grind for everything. He has got there through sheer hard work. That is why I was sure he would hold on and not choke on the last day."

Testimony to Oosthuizen's character also came from Els, whose Foundation had supported Oosthuizen for three years before he turned professional. Els, like Norman, was at home watching events unfold on television. "It would be difficult to find anybody in the

world who is more proud of him right now," Els said on Sunday evening. "I could not be happier. I thought he was going to be an exceptional player long before anybody had heard of him. He had a lot of natural ability plus he had length, which are important factors in the modern game. He shot a stunning 57 at Mossel Bay, which will never be equalled nor bettered."

Oosthuizen grew up on a dusty dairy farm in Albertina, not far from Mossel Bay, said to be one of the sunniest places in South Africa. Life was hard. There was not much money to be had from the family farm. He and his brother, both good tennis players, turned to golf at the local club, which had sand greens. Little did Louis know how learning to putt on those difficult surfaces would help him so well in years to come. At St Andrews he hardly missed a putt of less than seven feet all week. On Saturday he sank more than 150 feet of putts, including a tram-liner on the 16th. On Sunday it was more of the same, a 45-footer on the ninth helping to keep Paul Casey at bay.

Accuracy with the ball and control of it are two very important requirements if you are to do well over the Old Course. Patience is another. Oosthuizen had all three. He was the fourth longest driver, the most accurate player in the field from the tee, and the eighth most accurate in hitting the greens in the regulation figures. He took 121 putts (only Alejandro Canizares and Ricky Barnes with 120 were better) and was in only one bunker all week. He was in control from Friday morning and never let go.

Though he had luck with the weather with starting times of 11.52am on Thursday and 6.41am on Friday, Oosthuizen was not completely unaffected by the northwest wind that rose on Thursday afternoon and again on Friday afternoon. When it arose, he played through it as if it wasn't there. He knew how to do that, as Rupert had explained: "At Pinnacle Point near where he grew up they have a saying: 'You never open the back door if you have the front door open, otherwise the fridge will go flying out of the back door.'"

The Open Championship Results

Year	Champion	Score	Margin	Runners-up	Venue
1860	Willie Park Sr	174	2	Tom Morris Sr	Prestwick
1861	Tom Morris Sr	163	4	Willie Park Sr	Prestwick
1862	Tom Morris Sr	163	13	Willie Park Sr	Prestwick
1863	Willie Park Sr	168	2	Tom Morris Sr	Prestwick
1864	Tom Morris Sr	167	2	Andrew Strath	Prestwick
1865	Andrew Strath	162	2	Willie Park Sr	Prestwick
1866	Willie Park Sr	169	2	David Park	Prestwick
1867	Tom Morris Sr	170	2	Willie Park Sr	Prestwick
1868	Tommy Morris Jr	154	3	Tom Morris Sr	Prestwick
1869	Tommy Morris Jr	157	11	Bob Kirk	Prestwick
1870	Tommy Morris Jr	149	12	Bob Kirk, Davie Strath	Prestwick
1871	*No Competition*				
1872	Tommy Morris Jr	166	3	Davie Strath	Prestwick
1873	Tom Kidd	179	1	Jamie Anderson	St Andrews
1874	Mungo Park	159	2	Tommy Morris Jr	Musselburgh
1875	Willie Park Sr	166	2	Bob Martin	Prestwick
1876	Bob Martin	176	—	Davie Strath	St Andrews
	(Martin was awarded the title when Strath refused to play-off)				
1877	Jamie Anderson	160	2	Bob Pringle	Musselburgh
1878	Jamie Anderson	157	2	Bob Kirk	Prestwick
1879	Jamie Anderson	169	3	Jamie Allan, Andrew Kirkaldy	St Andrews
1880	Bob Ferguson	162	5	Peter Paxton	Musselburgh
1881	Bob Ferguson	170	3	Jamie Anderson	Prestwick
1882	Bob Ferguson	171	3	Willie Fernie	St Andrews
1883	Willie Fernie	158	Playoff	Bob Ferguson	Musselburgh
1884	Jack Simpson	160	4	Douglas Rolland, Willie Fernie	Prestwick
1885	Bob Martin	171	1	Archie Simpson	St Andrews
1886	David Brown	157	2	Willie Campbell	Musselburgh
1887	Willie Park Jr	161	1	Bob Martin	Prestwick
1888	Jack Burns	171	1	David Anderson Jr, Ben Sayers	St Andrews
1889	Willie Park Jr	155	Playoff	Andrew Kirkaldy	Musselburgh
1890	John Ball Jr*	164	3	Willie Fernie, Archie Simpson	Prestwick
1891	Hugh Kirkaldy	166	2	Willie Fernie, Andrew Kirkaldy	St Andrews
	(From 1892 the competition was extended to 72 holes)				
1892	Harold Hilton*	305	3	John Ball Jr*, Hugh Kirkaldy, Sandy Herd	Muirfield

Year	Champion	Score	Margin	Runners-up	Venue
1893	Willie Auchterlonie	322	2	John Laidlay*	Prestwick
1894	JH Taylor	326	5	Douglas Rolland	Royal St George's
1895	JH Taylor	322	4	Sandy Herd	St Andrews
1896	Harry Vardon	316	Playoff	JH Taylor	Muirfield
1897	Harold Hilton*	314	1	James Braid	Royal Liverpool
1898	Harry Vardon	307	1	Willie Park Jr	Prestwick
1899	Harry Vardon	310	5	Jack White	Royal St George's
1900	JH Taylor	309	8	Harry Vardon	St Andrews
1901	James Braid	309	3	Harry Vardon	Muirfield
1902	Sandy Herd	307	1	Harry Vardon, James Braid	Royal Liverpool
1903	Harry Vardon	300	6	Tom Vardon	Prestwick
1904	Jack White	296	1	James Braid, JH Taylor	Royal St George's
1905	James Braid	318	5	JH Taylor, Rowland Jones	St Andrews
1906	James Braid	300	4	JH Taylor	Muirfield
1907	Arnaud Massy	312	2	JH Taylor	Royal Liverpool
1908	James Braid	291	8	Tom Ball	Prestwick
1909	JH Taylor	295	6	James Braid, Tom Ball	Deal
1910	James Braid	299	4	Sandy Herd	St Andrews
1911	Harry Vardon	303	Playoff	Arnaud Massy	Royal St George's
1912	Ted Ray	295	4	Harry Vardon	Muirfield
1913	JH Taylor	304	8	Ted Ray	Royal Liverpool
1914	Harry Vardon	306	3	JH Taylor	Prestwick
1915-1919 *No Championship*					
1920	George Duncan	303	2	Sandy Herd	Deal
1921	Jock Hutchison	296	Playoff	Roger Wethered*	St Andrews
1922	Walter Hagen	300	1	George Duncan, Jim Barnes	Royal St George's
1923	Arthur G Havers	295	1	Walter Hagen	Troon
1924	Walter Hagen	301	1	Ernest Whitcombe	Royal Liverpool
1925	Jim Barnes	300	1	Archie Compston, Ted Ray	Prestwick
1926	Bobby Jones*	291	2	Al Watrous	Royal Lytham
1927	Bobby Jones*	285	6	Aubrey Boomer, Fred Robson	St Andrews
1928	Walter Hagen	292	2	Gene Sarazen	Royal St George's
1929	Walter Hagen	292	6	John Farrell	Muirfield
1930	Bobby Jones*	291	2	Leo Diegel, Macdonald Smith	Royal Liverpool
1931	Tommy Armour	296	1	Jose Jurado	Carnoustie
1932	Gene Sarazen	283	5	Macdonald Smith	Prince's
1933	Denny Shute	292	Playoff	Craig Wood	St Andrews
1934	Henry Cotton	283	5	Sid Brews	Royal St George's
1935	Alf Perry	283	4	Alf Padgham	Muirfield
1936	Alf Padgham	287	1	Jimmy Adams	Royal Liverpool
1937	Henry Cotton	290	2	Reg Whitcombe	Carnoustie
1938	Reg Whitcombe	295	2	Jimmy Adams	Royal St George's
1939	Richard Burton	290	2	Johnny Bulla	St Andrews
1940-1945 *No Championship*					
1946	Sam Snead	290	4	Bobby Locke, Johnny Bulla	St Andrews
1947	Fred Daly	293	1	Reg Horne, Frank Stranahan*	Royal Liverpool
1948	Henry Cotton	284	5	Fred Daly	Muirfield
1949	Bobby Locke	283	Playoff	Harry Bradshaw	Royal St George's
1950	Bobby Locke	279	2	Roberto de Vicenzo	Troon
1951	Max Faulkner	285	2	Antonio Cerda	Royal Portrush
1952	Bobby Locke	287	1	Peter Thomson	Royal Lytham
1953	Ben Hogan	282	4	Frank Stranahan*, Dai Rees, Peter Thomson, Antonio Cerda	Carnoustie

Past Open Champions in attendance were (first row, left to right): Tom Weiskopf, Tony Jacklin, Bob Charles, Gary Player, Stewart Cink, Colin M Brown (Captain of the R&A), Peter Thomson, Arnold Palmer, Robert de Vicenzo, Lee Trevino, Tom Watson;

Year	Champion	Score	Margin	Runners-up	Venue
1954	Peter Thomson	283	1	Syd Scott, Dai Rees, Bobby Locke	Royal Birkdale
1955	Peter Thomson	281	2	John Fallon	St Andrews
1956	Peter Thomson	286	3	Flory van Donck	Royal Liverpool
1957	Bobby Locke	279	3	Peter Thomson	St Andrews
1958	Peter Thomson	278	Playoff	Dave Thomas	Royal Lytham
1959	Gary Player	284	2	Flory van Donck, Fred Bullock	Muirfield
1960	Kel Nagle	278	1	Arnold Palmer	St Andrews
1961	Arnold Palmer	284	1	Dai Rees	Royal Birkdale
1962	Arnold Palmer	276	6	Kel Nagle	Troon
1963	Bob Charles	277	Playoff	Phil Rodgers	Royal Lytham
1964	Tony Lema	279	5	Jack Nicklaus	St Andrews
1965	Peter Thomson	285	2	Christy O'Connor, Brian Huggett	Royal Birkdale
1966	Jack Nicklaus	282	1	Dave Thomas, Doug Sanders	Muirfield
1967	Roberto de Vicenzo	278	2	Jack Nicklaus	Royal Liverpool
1968	Gary Player	289	2	Jack Nicklaus, Bob Charles	Carnoustie
1969	Tony Jacklin	280	2	Bob Charles	Royal Lytham
1970	Jack Nicklaus	283	Playoff	Doug Sanders	St Andrews
1971	Lee Trevino	278	1	Lu Liang Huan	Royal Birkdale
1972	Lee Trevino	278	1	Jack Nicklaus	Muirfield
1973	Tom Weiskopf	276	3	Neil Coles, Johnny Miller	Troon
1974	Gary Player	282	4	Peter Oosterhuis	Royal Lytham
1975	Tom Watson	279	Playoff	Jack Newton	Carnoustie
1976	Johnny Miller	279	6	Jack Nicklaus, Seve Ballesteros	Royal Birkdale
1977	Tom Watson	268	1	Jack Nicklaus	Turnberry
1978	Jack Nicklaus	281	2	Simon Owen, Ben Crenshaw, Ray Floyd, Tom Kite	St Andrews
1979	Seve Ballesteros	283	3	Jack Nicklaus, Ben Crenshaw	Royal Lytham
1980	Tom Watson	271	4	Lee Trevino	Muirfield
1981	Bill Rogers	276	4	Bernhard Langer	Royal St George's
1982	Tom Watson	284	1	Peter Oosterhuis, Nick Price	Royal Troon
1983	Tom Watson	275	1	Hale Irwin, Andy Bean	Royal Birkdale

(second row): Ben Curtis, Tom Lehman, Mark O'Meara, Justin Leonard, Todd Hamilton, David Duval, Paul Lawrie, Mark Calcavecchia, Ian Baker-Finch, Ernie Els, Sir Nick Faldo, Padraig Harrington, John Daly, Tiger Woods, Bill Rogers, Sandy Lyle.

Year	Champion	Score	Margin	Runners-up	Venue
1984	Seve Ballesteros	276	2	Bernhard Langer, Tom Watson	St Andrews
1985	Sandy Lyle	282	1	Payne Stewart	Royal St George's
1986	Greg Norman	280	5	Gordon J Brand	Turnberry
1987	Nick Faldo	279	1	Rodger Davis, Paul Azinger	Muirfield
1988	Seve Ballesteros	273	2	Nick Price	Royal Lytham
1989	Mark Calcavecchia	275	Playoff	Greg Norman, Wayne Grady	Royal Troon
1990	Nick Faldo	270	5	Mark McNulty, Payne Stewart	St Andrews
1991	Ian Baker-Finch	272	2	Mike Harwood	Royal Birkdale
1992	Nick Faldo	272	1	John Cook	Muirfield
1993	Greg Norman	267	2	Nick Faldo	Royal St George's
1994	Nick Price	268	1	Jesper Parnevik	Turnberry
1995	John Daly	282	Playoff	Costantino Rocca	St Andrews
1996	Tom Lehman	271	2	Mark McCumber, Ernie Els	Royal Lytham
1997	Justin Leonard	272	3	Jesper Parnevik, Darren Clarke	Royal Troon
1998	Mark O'Meara	280	Playoff	Brian Watts	Royal Birkdale
1999	Paul Lawrie	290	Playoff	Justin Leonard, Jean Van de Velde	Carnoustie
2000	Tiger Woods	269	8	Ernie Els, Thomas Bjorn	St Andrews
2001	David Duval	274	3	Niclas Fasth	Royal Lytham
2002	Ernie Els	278	Playoff	Thomas Levet, Stuart Appleby, Steve Elkington	Muirfield
2003	Ben Curtis	283	1	Thomas Bjorn, Vijay Singh	Royal St George's
2004	Todd Hamilton	274	Playoff	Ernie Els	Royal Troon
2005	Tiger Woods	274	5	Colin Montgomerie	St Andrews
2006	Tiger Woods	270	2	Chris DiMarco	Royal Liverpool
2007	Padraig Harrington	277	Playoff	Sergio Garcia	Carnoustie
2008	Padraig Harrington	283	4	Ian Poulter	Royal Birkdale
2009	Stewart Cink	278	Playoff	Tom Watson	Turnberry
2010	Louis Oosthuizen	272	7	Lee Westwood	St Andrews

*Denotes amateurs

The Open Championship Records

Most Victories

6: Harry Vardon, 1896, 1898, 1899, 1903, 1911, 1914
5: James Braid, 1901, 1905, 1906, 1908, 1910; JH Taylor, 1894, 1895, 1900, 1909, 1913; Peter Thomson, 1954, 1955, 1956, 1958, 1965; Tom Watson, 1975, 1977, 1980, 1982, 1983

Most Runner-Up or Joint Runner-Up Finishes

7: Jack Nicklaus, 1964, 1967, 1968, 1972, 1976, 1977, 1979
6: JH Taylor, 1896, 1904, 1905, 1906, 1907, 1914

Oldest Winners

Tom Morris Sr, 1867, 46 years 99 days
Roberto de Vicenzo, 1967, 44 years 93 days
Harry Vardon, 1914, 44 years 41 days

Youngest Winners

Tommy Morris Jr, 1868, 17 years 5 months 3 days
Willie Auchterlonie, 1893, 21 years 24 days
Seve Ballesteros, 1979, 22 years 3 months 12 days

Known Oldest and Youngest Competitors

74 years, 11 months, 24 days: Tom Morris Sr, 1896
74 years, 4 months, 9 days: Gene Sarazen, 1976
Tommy Morris Jr, 1865, 14 years 4 months 25 days, 1865

Largest Margin of Victory

13 strokes, Tom Morris Sr, 1862
12 strokes, Tommy Morris Jr, 1870
11 strokes, Tommy Morris Jr, 1869
8 strokes, JH Taylor, 1900 and 1913; James Braid, 1908; Tiger Woods, 2000

Lowest Winning Total by a Champion

267, Greg Norman, Royal St George's 1993 – 66, 68, 69, 64
268, Tom Watson, Turnberry, 1977 – 69, 66, 67, 66; Nick Price, Turnberry, 1994 – 69, 66, 67, 66
269, Tiger Woods, St Andrews, 2000 – 67, 66, 67, 69

Lowest Total in Relation to Par Since 1963

19 under par: Tiger Woods, St Andrews, 2000 (269)
18 under par: Nick Faldo, St Andrews, 1990 (270); Tiger Woods, Royal Liverpool, 2006 (270)

Lowest Total by a Runner-Up

269: Jack Nicklaus, Turnberry, 1977 – 68, 70, 65, 66; Nick Faldo, Royal St George's, 1993 – 69, 63, 70, 67; Jesper Parnevik, Turnberry, 1994 – 68, 66, 68, 67

Lowest Total by an Amateur

281: Iain Pyman, Royal St George's, 1993 – 68, 72, 70, 71; Tiger Woods, Royal Lytham & St Annes, 1996 – 75, 66, 70, 70

Lowest Individual Round

63: Mark Hayes, second round, Turnberry, 1977; Isao Aoki, third round, Muirfield, 1980; Greg Norman, second round, Turnberry, 1986; Paul Broadhurst, third round, St Andrews, 1990; Jodie Mudd, fourth round, Royal Birkdale, 1991; Nick Faldo, second round, Royal St George's, 1993; Payne Stewart, fourth round, Royal St George's, 1993; Rory McIlroy, first round, St Andrews, 2010

Lowest Individual Round by an Amateur

66: Frank Stranahan, fourth round, Troon, 1950; Tiger Woods, second round, Royal Lytham & St Annes, 1996; Justin Rose, second round, Royal Birkdale, 1998

Lowest First Round

63: Rory McIlroy, St Andrews, 2010

Lowest Second Round

63: Mark Hayes, Turnberry, 1977; Greg Norman, Turnberry, 1986; Nick Faldo, Royal St George's, 1993

Lowest Third Round

63: Isao Aoki, Muirfield, 1980; Paul Broadhurst, St Andrews, 1990

Lowest Fourth Round

63: Jodie Mudd, Royal Birkdale, 1991; Payne Stewart, Royal St George's, 1993

Lowest Score over the First 36 Holes

130: Nick Faldo, Muirfield, 1992 – 66, 64

Lowest Score over the Middle 36 Holes

130: Fuzzy Zoeller, Turnberry, 1994 – 66, 64

Lowest Score over the Final 36 Holes

130: Tom Watson, Turnberry, 1977 – 65, 65; Ian Baker-Finch, Royal Birkdale, 1991 – 64, 66; Anders Forsbrand, Turnberry, 1994 – 66, 64

Lowest Score over the First 54 Holes

198: Tom Lehman, Royal Lytham & St Annes, 1996 – 67, 67, 64
199: Nick Faldo, St Andrews, 1990 – 67, 65, 67; Nick Faldo, Muirfield, 1992 – 66, 64, 69

Lowest Score over the Final 54 Holes

199: Nick Price, Turnberry, 1994 – 66, 67, 66

Lowest Score for Nine Holes

28: Denis Durnian, first nine, Royal Birkdale, 1983
29: Tom Haliburton, first nine, Royal Lytham & St Annes, 1963; Peter Thomson, first nine, Royal Lytham & St Annes, 1963; Tony Jacklin, first nine, St Andrews, 1970; Bill Longmuir, first nine, Royal Lytham & St Annes, 1979; David J Russell first nine, Royal Lytham & St Annes, 1988; Ian Baker-Finch, first nine, St Andrews, 1990; Paul Broadhurst, first nine, St Andrews, 1990; Ian Baker-Finch, first nine, Royal Birkdale, 1991; Paul McGinley, first nine, Royal Lytham & St Annes, 1996; Ernie Els, first nine, Muirfield, 2002; Sergio Garcia, first nine, Royal Liverpool, 2006

Most Successive Victories

4: Tommy Morris Jr, 1868-72 *(No Championship in 1871)*
3: Jamie Anderson, 1877-79; Bob Ferguson, 1880-82; Peter Thomson, 1954-56
2: Tom Morris Sr, 1861-62; JH Taylor, 1894-95; Harry Vardon, 1898-99; James Braid, 1905-06; Bobby Jones, 1926-27; Walter Hagen, 1928-29; Bobby Locke, 1949-50; Arnold Palmer, 1961-62; Lee Trevino, 1971-72; Tom Watson, 1982-83; Tiger Woods, 2005-06; Padraig Harrington, 2007-08

Amateurs Who Have Won The Open

3: Bobby Jones, Royal Lytham & St Annes, 1926; St Andrews, 1927; Royal Liverpool, 1930
2: Harold Hilton, Muirfield, 1892; Royal Liverpool, 1897
1: John Ball Jr, Prestwick, 1890

On Tuesday, the University of St Andrews presented honorary degrees to (from left) Tom Watson, Arnold Palmer, and Padraig Harrington.

Champions Who Won on Debut

Willie Park Sr, Prestwick, 1860; Tom Kidd, St Andrews, 1873; Mungo Park, Musselburgh, 1874; Jock Hutchison, St Andrews, 1921; Denny Shute, St Andrews, 1933; Ben Hogan, Carnoustie, 1953; Tony Lema, St Andrews, 1964; Tom Watson, Carnoustie, 1975; Ben Curtis, Royal St George's, 2003

Greatest Interval Between First and Last Victory

19 years: JH Taylor, 1894-1913
18 years: Harry Vardon, 1896-1914
15 years: Willie Park Sr, 1860-75; Gary Player, 1959-74
14 years: Henry Cotton, 1934-48

Greatest Interval Between Victories

11 years: Henry Cotton, 1937-48 *(No Championship 1940-45)*
9 years: Willie Park Sr, 1866-75; Bob Martin, 1876-85; JH Taylor, 1900-09; Gary Player, 1959-68

Sir Nick Faldo (1987, 1990, 1992) | **John Daly (1995)** | **Tiger Woods (2000, 2005, 2006)**

Champions Who Have Won in Three Separate Decades

Harry Vardon, 1896, 1898 & 1899/1903/1911 & 1914
JH Taylor, 1894 & 1895/1900 & 1909/1913
Gary Player, 1959, 1968, 1974

Competitors with the Most Top Five Finishes

16: JH Taylor; Jack Nicklaus

Competitors Who Have Recorded the Most Rounds Under Par From 1963

59: Jack Nicklaus
53: Nick Faldo

Competitors with the Most Finishes Under Par From 1963

14: Jack Nicklaus; Nick Faldo
13: Ernie Els; Tom Watson

Champions Who Have Led Outright After Every Round

72 hole Championships
Ted Ray, 1912; Bobby Jones, 1927; Gene Sarazen, 1932; Henry Cotton, 1934; Tom Weiskopf, 1973; Tiger Woods, 2005
36 hole Championships
Willie Park Sr, 1860 and 1866; Tom Morris Sr, 1862 and 1864; Tommy Morris Jr, 1869 and 1870; Mungo Park, 1874; Jamie Anderson, 1879; Bob Ferguson, 1880, 1881, 1882; Willie Fernie, 1883; Jack Simpson, 1884; Hugh Kirkaldy, 1891

Largest Leads Since 1892

After 18 holes:
5 strokes: Sandy Herd, 1896
4 strokes: Harry Vardon, 1902; Jim Barnes, 1925; Christy O'Connor Jr, 1985
After 36 holes:
9 strokes: Henry Cotton, 1934
6 strokes: Abe Mitchell, 1920
After 54 holes:
10 strokes: Henry Cotton, 1934
7 strokes: Harry Vardon, 1903; Tony Lema, 1964
6 strokes: JH Taylor, 1900; James Braid, 1905; James Braid, 1908; Max Faulkner, 1951; Tom Lehman, 1996; Tiger Woods, 2000

Champions Who Had Four Rounds, Each Better than the One Before

Jack White, Royal St George's, 1904 – 80, 75, 72, 69
James Braid, Muirfield, 1906 – 77, 76, 74, 73
Ben Hogan, Carnoustie, 1953 – 73, 71, 70, 68
Gary Player, Muirfield, 1959 – 75, 71, 70, 68

Same Number of Strokes in Each of the Four Rounds by a Champion

Denny Shute, St Andrews, 1933 – 73, 73, 73, 73 (excluding the playoff)

Best 18-Hole Recovery by a Champion

George Duncan, Deal, 1920. Duncan was 13 strokes behind the leader, Abe Mitchell, after 36 holes and level with him after 54.

Greatest Variation Between Rounds by a Champion

14 strokes: Henry Cotton, 1934, second round 65, fourth round 79
12 strokes: Henry Cotton, 1934, first round 67, fourth round 79
11 strokes: Jack White, 1904, first round 80, fourth round 69; Greg Norman, 1986, first round 74, second round 63; Greg Norman, 1986, second round 63, third round 74
10 strokes: Seve Ballesteros, 1979, second round 65, third round 75

Greatest Variation Between Two Successive Rounds by a Champion

11 strokes: Greg Norman, 1986, first round 74, second round 63; Greg Norman, 1986, second round 63, third round 74
10 strokes: Seve Ballesteros, 1979, second round 65, third round 75

Greatest Comeback by a Champion

After 18 holes
Harry Vardon, 1896, 11 strokes behind the leader
After 36 holes
George Duncan, 1920, 13 strokes behind the leader
After 54 holes
Paul Lawrie, 1999, 10 strokes behind the leader

Champions Who Had Four Rounds Under 70

Greg Norman, Royal St George's, 1993 – 66, 68, 69, 64; Nick Price, Turnberry, 1994 – 69, 66, 67, 66; Tiger Woods, St Andrews, 2000 – 67, 66, 67, 69

Competitors Who Failed to Win The Open Despite Having Four Rounds Under 70

Ernie Els, Royal St George's, 1993 – 68, 69, 69, 68; Jesper Parnevik, Turnberry, 1994 – 68, 66, 68, 67; Ernie Els, Royal Troon, 2004 – 69, 69, 68, 68

Lowest Final Round by a Champion

64: Greg Norman, Royal St George's, 1993
65: Tom Watson, Turnberry, 1977; Seve Ballesteros, Royal Lytham & St Annes, 1988; Justin Leonard, Royal Troon, 1997

Worst Round by a Champion (Since 1939)

78: Fred Daly, third round, Royal Liverpool, 1947
76: Bobby Locke, second round, Royal St George's, 1949; Paul Lawrie, third round, Carnoustie, 1999

Champion with the Worst Finishing Round (Since 1939)

75: Sam Snead, St Andrews, 1946

Lowest Opening Round by a Champion

65: Louis Oosthuizen, St Andrews, 2010

Most Open Championship Appearances

46: Gary Player
38: Jack Nicklaus

Most Final Day Appearances (Since 1892)

32: Jack Nicklaus
31: Sandy Herd
30: JH Taylor
28: Ted Ray
27: Harry Vardon; James Braid; Nick Faldo
26: Peter Thomson; Gary Player

Most Appearances by a Champion Before His First Victory

15: Nick Price, 1994
14: Sandy Herd, 1902
13: Ted Ray, 1912; Jack White, 1904; Reg Whitcombe, 1938; Mark O'Meara, 1998
11: George Duncan, 1920; Nick Faldo, 1987; Ernie Els, 2002; Stewart Cink, 2009
10: Roberto de Vicenzo, 1967; Padraig Harrington, 2007

The Open Which Provided the Greatest Number of Rounds Under 70 Since 1946

148 rounds, Turnberry, 1994

The Open with the Fewest Rounds Under 70 Since 1946

2 rounds, St Andrews, 1946; Royal Liverpool, 1947; Carnoustie, 1968

Statistically Most Difficult Hole Since 1982

St Andrews, 1984, Par-4 17th, 4.79

Longest Course in Open History

Carnoustie, 2007, 7,421 yards

Number of Times Each Course Has Hosted The Open Championship

St Andrews, 28; Prestwick, 24; Muirfield, 15; Royal St George's, 13; Royal Liverpool, 11; Royal Lytham & St Annes, 10; Royal Birkdale, 9; Royal Troon, 8; Carnoustie, 7; Musselburgh, 6; Turnberry, 4; Royal Cinque Ports, 2; Royal Portrush and Prince's, 1

Prize Money

Year	Total	First Prize
1860	nil	nil
1863	10	nil
1864	15	6
1865	20	8
1866	11	6
1867	16	7
1868	12	6
1872	unknown	8
1873	unknown	11
1874	20	8
1876	27	10
1877	20	8
1878	unknown	8
1879	47	10
1880	unknown	8
1881	21	8
1882	47.25	12
1883	20	8
1884	23	8
1885	35.50	10
1886	20	8
1889	22	8
1890	29.50	13
1891	28.50	10
1892	110	35
1893	100	30
1900	125	50
1910	135	50
1920	225	75
1927	275	75
1930	400	100
1931	500	100
1946	1,000	150
1949	1,500	300
1951	1,700	300
1953	2,500	500
1954	3,500	750
1955	3,750	1,000
1958	4,850	1,000
1959	5,000	1,000
1960	7,000	1,250
1961	8,500	1,400
1963	8,500	1,500
1965	10,000	1,750
1966	15,000	2,100
1968	20,000	3,000
1969	30,000	4,250
1970	40,000	5,250
1971	45,000	5,500
1972	50,000	5,500
1975	75,000	7,500
1977	100,000	10,000
1978	125,000	12,500
1979	155,000	15,000

Year	Total	First Prize
1980	200,000	25,000
1982	250,000	32,000
1983	310,000	40,000
1984	451,000	55,000
1985	530,000	65,000
1986	600,000	70,000
1987	650,000	75,000
1988	700,000	80,000
1989	750,000	80,000
1990	825,000	85,000
1991	900,000	90,000
1992	950,000	95,000
1993	1,000,000	100,000

Year	Total	First Prize
1994	1,100,000	110,000
1995	1,250,000	125,000
1996	1,400,000	200,000
1997	1,600,000	250,000
1998	1,800,000	300,000
1999	2,000,000	350,000
2000	2,750,000	500,000
2001	3,300,000	600,000
2002	3,800,000	700,000
2003	3,900,000	700,000
2004	4,000,000	720,000
2007	4,200,000	750,000
2010	4,800,000	850,000

Attendance

Year	Total	Year	Total	Year	Total
1962	37,098	1979	134,501	1996	170,000
1963	24,585	1980	131,610	1997	176,000
1964	35,954	1981	111,987	1998	195,100
1965	32,927	1982	133,299	1999	157,000
1966	40,182	1983	142,892	2000	230,000
1967	29,880	1984	193,126	2001	178,000
1968	51,819	1985	141,619	2002	161,500
1969	46,001	1986	134,261	2003	183,000
1970	81,593	1987	139,189	2004	176,000
1971	70,076	1988	191,334	2005	223,000
1972	84,746	1989	160,639	2006	230,000
1973	78,810	1990	208,680	2007	154,000
1974	92,796	1991	189,435	2008	201,500
1975	85,258	1992	146,427	2009	123,000
1976	92,021	1993	141,000	2010	201,000
1977	87,615	1994	128,000		
1978	125,271	1995	180,000		

The 139th Open Championship

Complete Scores

HOLE			1	2	3	4	5	6	7	8	9	10	11	12	13	14	15	16	17	18	
PAR		POSITION	4	4	4	4	5	4	4	3	4	4	3	4	4	5	4	4	4	4	TOTAL
Louis Oosthuizen	2	Round 1	4	4	4	3	4	4	3	2	3	3	3	4	4	4	3	4	5	4	65
South Africa	1	Round 2	4	4	4	4	4	3	3	3	4	3	4	3	5	4	4	4	4	3	67
£850,000	1	Round 3	5	4	4	4	5	4	3	3	3	4	3	4	4	5	4	3	4	3	69
	1	Round 4	4	4	4	4	5	4	4	4	2	4	3	3	4	5	4	4	5	4	**71 -272**
Lee Westwood	T8	Round 1	4	4	4	4	4	3	3	2	3	4	3	4	5	4	4	4	4	4	67
England	T3	Round 2	4	4	4	4	4	4	4	3	4	4	3	4	4	5	4	4	4	4	71
£500,000	T4	Round 3	4	4	4	5	5	5	4	3	4	3	2	4	4	4	5	4	4	3	71
	2	Round 4	4	4	4	4	5	4	4	3	3	4	3	5	3	4	4	4	5	3	**70 -279**
Rory McIlroy	1	Round 1	4	4	3	4	5	4	4	3	2	3	2	3	4	4	3	4	4	3	63
Northern Ireland	T38	Round 2	4	4	4	5	5	5	5	4	4	4	5	4	5	5	5	4	4	4	80
£256,667	T12	Round 3	4	4	4	4	4	5	4	2	3	4	3	3	4	5	3	4	6	3	69
	T3	Round 4	4	4	4	4	4	4	4	3	3	4	4	3	4	4	4	4	4	3	**68 -280**
Henrik Stenson	T17	Round 1	4	4	3	4	5	4	3	3	3	4	2	4	4	5	4	4	4	4	68
Sweden	T28	Round 2	4	5	4	4	4	5	4	4	4	4	4	4	4	5	4	4	4	3	74
£256,667	T4	Round 3	3	4	4	4	4	4	2	3	4	3	4	2	5	4	4	5	5	3	67
	T3	Round 4	4	4	4	4	5	4	3	3	4	3	4	4	4	5	4	4	4	4	**71 -280**
Paul Casey	T30	Round 1	3	5	4	4	4	3	4	4	3	4	3	4	4	5	4	4	4	3	69
England	T3	Round 2	3	3	3	4	5	3	4	2	4	4	3	4	4	5	4	4	7	3	69
£256,667	2	Round 3	4	3	3	4	4	4	3	3	3	4	3	4	4	5	4	4	4	4	67
	T3	Round 4	4	5	4	4	5	3	4	3	3	4	3	7	4	5	5	4	4	4	**75 -280**
Retief Goosen	T30	Round 1	3	3	5	4	4	5	3	3	4	4	3	4	4	5	4	4	4	3	69
South Africa	T7	Round 2	4	4	4	4	4	3	4	3	4	3	4	4	4	5	4	4	4	4	70
£175,000	T8	Round 3	4	5	4	4	4	4	3	3	4	3	4	4	4	5	4	4	6	3	72
	6	Round 4	4	4	4	4	4	4	4	3	4	4	3	4	4	5	4	4	4	3	**70 -281**
Robert Rock	T17	Round 1	5	3	4	4	4	4	3	3	4	4	3	3	4	4	4	4	4	4	68
England	T68	Round 2	4	4	4	4	5	4	5	4	3	5	4	5	5	5	5	4	4	4	78
£121,250	T18	Round 3	3	4	4	4	5	3	2	3	3	4	3	4	4	5	4	4	5	3	67
	T7	Round 4	4	4	4	4	4	3	4	4	3	4	4	4	4	4	4	4	4	3	**69 -282**
Sean O'Hair	T8	Round 1	3	3	3	4	5	3	3	3	3	4	3	4	4	5	4	4	5	4	67
USA	T7	Round 2	5	5	4	4	4	4	4	4	4	3	4	4	4	5	4	4	3	4	72
£121,250	T8	Round 3	4	4	5	4	6	4	3	5	4	3	3	5	4	4	4	4	4	3	72
	T7	Round 4	4	4	4	4	5	3	4	3	4	3	3	4	6	4	4	4	5	3	**71 -282**

* Denotes amateurs

HOLE			1	2	3	4	5	6	7	8	9	10	11	12	13	14	15	16	17	18	
PAR	POSITION		4	4	4	4	5	4	4	3	4	4	3	4	4	5	4	4	4	4	TOTAL
Nick Watney	T8	Round 1	4	4	3	4	5	4	3	3	3	3	3	4	4	4	4	4	4	4	67
USA	T14	Round 2	5	4	4	4	5	4	3	3	4	4	4	4	4	5	4	4	4	4	73
£121,250	T8	Round 3	4	5	3	3	5	5	5	3	3	4	4	4	4	5	3	4	4	3	71
	T7	Round 4	4	4	4	5	6	4	4	3	3	3	3	5	3	5	4	4	4	3	71 -**282**
Martin Kaymer	T30	Round 1	3	4	4	4	5	4	4	3	4	4	3	4	3	5	4	4	4	3	69
Germany	T14	Round 2	4	4	4	4	4	4	4	4	3	3	3	4	4	5	5	5	4	3	71
£121,250	3	Round 3	4	4	3	3	5	4	4	3	5	3	3	3	5	4	4	4	4	3	68
	T7	Round 4	5	4	4	4	5	3	4	2	4	5	3	5	4	4	3	5	5	5	74 -**282**
Alvaro Quiros	T74	Round 1	3	4	4	4	5	4	3	4	4	4	3	4	5	5	4	4	4	4	72
Spain	T28	Round 2	4	4	4	3	4	4	5	2	3	4	3	4	3	5	5	4	5	4	70
£81,667	T41	Round 3	4	5	4	5	5	4	4	3	3	5	3	4	4	4	5	4	5	3	74
	T11	Round 4	4	4	4	3	4	4	3	3	3	3	3	3	4	6	4	4	4	3	67 -**283**
Jeff Overton	T97	Round 1	4	4	4	4	5	4	4	3	3	5	3	4	4	6	4	3	5	4	73
USA	T28	Round 2	4	3	4	3	5	4	4	3	4	4	3	4	5	3	4	4	4	4	69
£81,667	T26	Round 3	4	4	4	3	5	4	4	3	3	5	4	5	4	4	4	4	4	4	72
	T11	Round 4	3	4	4	4	5	4	4	3	4	4	3	4	4	4	4	5	4	3	69 -**283**
Luke Donald	T97	Round 1	4	4	4	4	5	4	4	4	4	4	3	4	4	4	4	4	5	4	73
England	T56	Round 2	4	5	4	4	5	4	3	3	3	4	3	4	4	5	5	4	5	3	72
£81,667	T26	Round 3	4	4	4	4	4	4	4	2	4	4	3	3	4	6	3	5	4	3	69
	T11	Round 4	5	4	3	5	5	4	4	3	4	3	3	5	4	4	4	4	3	2	69 -**283**
Rickie Fowler	T149	Round 1	4	4	5	4	4	4	5	4	3	4	3	5	4	4	5	7	6	4	79
USA	T68	Round 2	4	3	3	4	4	4	4	3	3	4	3	4	5	5	3	4	4	3	67
£57,188	T52	Round 3	4	4	4	4	5	4	3	3	3	4	3	4	4	5	4	4	5	4	71
	T14	Round 4	4	4	3	4	5	4	4	3	4	4	3	4	3	4	4	4	3	3	67 -**284**
Tom Lehman	T59	Round 1	4	3	3	4	6	3	4	3	4	3	4	3	5	5	5	4	4	4	71
USA	T7	Round 2	4	4	4	4	5	4	4	2	4	4	3	3	4	4	4	4	4	3	68
£57,188	T26	Round 3	4	4	4	4	5	5	4	3	4	4	3	4	4	6	4	5	4	4	75
	T14	Round 4	4	4	4	4	5	4	4	3	4	4	3	4	4	5	3	4	5	2	70 -**284**
Charl Schwartzel	T59	Round 1	4	6	4	4	6	4	5	3	4	3	2	4	4	4	4	4	3	3	71
South Africa	T68	Round 2	4	4	3	5	6	4	4	3	4	4	3	4	5	5	4	4	5	4	75
£57,188	T26	Round 3	4	4	4	3	4	4	3	3	3	4	3	5	4	4	4	4	4	3	68
	T14	Round 4	4	4	4	4	4	5	4	3	3	4	3	4	4	5	4	4	4	3	70 -**284**
Ignacio Garrido	T30	Round 1	3	4	3	5	4	4	4	3	4	4	3	4	5	4	4	4	4	4	69
Spain	T14	Round 2	4	4	5	4	5	4	4	2	4	4	3	5	4	4	4	4	3	4	71
£57,188	T18	Round 3	4	4	4	5	5	4	4	2	4	5	4	4	4	4	4	3	6	3	73
	T14	Round 4	4	3	4	4	5	4	3	3	4	4	3	6	5	4	4	4	4	3	71 -**284**
Jin Jeong*	T17	Round 1	3	4	4	3	4	3	4	3	4	4	3	3	4	4	4	5	4	5	68
South Korea	T3	Round 2	4	4	4	4	4	4	3	4	4	4	3	4	4	4	5	4	4	3	70
	T12	Round 3	4	4	4	5	3	4	5	3	5	4	3	4	4	5	4	5	5	3	74
	T14	Round 4	4	4	4	5	5	4	3	3	4	5	3	5	4	5	3	4	5	2	72 -**284**
Robert Karlsson	T30	Round 1	4	3	4	4	4	4	3	3	4	3	3	4	5	4	4	4	5	4	69
Sweden	T14	Round 2	3	4	4	4	4	4	4	3	3	4	3	4	6	5	4	4	5	3	71
£57,188	T12	Round 3	3	4	4	4	4	4	3	3	4	5	3	4	5	5	4	5	4	4	72
	T14	Round 4	3	3	4	5	5	4	4	3	4	4	3	4	4	5	4	4	5	4	72 -**284**
Sergio Garcia	T59	Round 1	4	5	3	5	4	3	4	3	4	4	3	4	4	4	4	5	4	4	71
Spain	T28	Round 2	4	3	4	5	4	4	3	3	3	5	3	4	4	4	5	4	5	4	71
£57,188	T12	Round 3	4	5	4	4	3	3	4	3	4	4	3	4	4	5	4	4	5	4	70
	T14	Round 4	4	4	4	4	4	5	3	3	4	4	3	4	4	5	4	5	5	3	72 -**284**

HOLE			1	2	3	4	5	6	7	8	9	10	11	12	13	14	15	16	17	18	
PAR	**POSITION**		4	4	4	4	5	4	4	3	4	4	3	4	4	5	4	4	4	4	**TOTAL**
JB Holmes	T46	Round 1	3	4	4	4	5	4	3	3	3	4	3	3	4	5	4	4	6	4	70
USA	T28	Round 2	5	4	5	3	4	4	4	3	4	4	4	4	4	5	3	4	5	3	72
£57,188	T12	Round 3	4	4	4	4	3	4	4	4	3	4	3	4	4	5	4	4	5	3	70
	T14	Round 4	4	4	4	4	5	5	3	2	4	4	3	3	4	5	5	4	5	4	72 -**284**
Dustin Johnson	T30	Round 1	3	3	4	3	5	4	4	3	4	4	4	4	4	5	4	3	4	4	69
USA	T21	Round 2	4	6	4	4	4	3	4	3	4	3	3	6	4	5	4	4	4	3	72
£57,188	7	Round 3	4	4	4	4	4	4	4	3	4	4	3	3	4	5	5	4	3	3	69
	T14	Round 4	4	4	4	4	6	4	4	4	2	4	3	4	4	4	5	3	6	5	74 -**284**
Trevor Immelman	T17	Round 1	4	4	4	4	5	3	3	3	3	3	3	5	3	5	4	4	4	4	68
South Africa	T28	Round 2	4	4	5	3	5	5	4	3	4	3	4	5	5	4	4	5	4	3	74
£42,000	T52	Round 3	4	5	4	5	4	5	3	4	4	5	3	4	4	5	4	4	5	3	75
	T23	Round 4	4	4	4	3	4	4	3	3	4	4	3	4	4	4	4	4	5	3	68 -**285**
Graeme McDowell	T59	Round 1	5	4	3	4	5	4	5	3	4	4	3	4	4	4	4	4	4	3	71
Northern Ireland	T7	Round 2	3	4	5	5	4	4	3	2	3	4	3	5	4	5	4	3	4	3	68
£42,000	T38	Round 3	4	5	4	5	5	4	4	3	4	3	4	3	5	5	4	4	5	6	76
	T23	Round 4	3	5	4	3	4	4	4	3	3	3	3	5	3	5	4	5	6	3	70 -**285**
Stephen Gallacher	T59	Round 1	3	4	4	4	4	4	4	3	4	3	3	4	3	4	5	4	5	6	71
Scotland	T43	Round 2	5	5	3	3	5	3	4	4	4	4	5	2	4	5	5	4	4	4	73
£42,000	T26	Round 3	4	4	4	4	5	4	3	3	3	4	2	3	4	6	4	4	5	4	70
	T23	Round 4	4	4	4	5	5	4	4	3	4	3	3	3	4	4	4	4	6	4	71 -**285**
Tiger Woods	T8	Round 1	4	3	4	4	5	4	3	3	3	4	3	3	3	4	4	4	5	4	67
USA	T14	Round 2	5	5	4	4	4	4	4	3	4	3	4	3	4	5	5	5	4	3	73
£42,000	T18	Round 3	4	4	4	4	6	4	4	4	3	4	3	3	5	5	3	4	5	4	73
	T23	Round 4	3	4	3	6	5	4	6	3	3	4	3	3	5	5	4	4	4	3	72 -**285**
Edoardo Molinari	T30	Round 1	4	4	4	4	5	3	4	3	4	3	3	3	4	4	5	4	4	4	69
Italy	T56	Round 2	4	4	4	5	5	4	4	3	3	4	3	4	5	5	5	5	5	4	76
£31,250	T65	Round 3	4	5	4	4	5	4	4	3	3	5	3	3	4	5	4	4	5	4	73
	T27	Round 4	4	4	3	4	4	4	4	3	4	3	4	4	4	4	4	4	5	3	68 -**286**
Matt Kuchar	T74	Round 1	4	4	4	3	4	5	4	3	3	4	3	5	4	6	4	4	4	4	72
USA	T68	Round 2	4	4	3	5	4	4	4	3	4	5	4	4	4	5	4	5	4	4	74
£31,250	T52	Round 3	4	4	4	5	5	4	3	3	4	4	2	4	4	4	4	5	4	4	71
	T27	Round 4	3	4	3	4	4	4	4	3	3	4	4	5	4	5	4	4	5	2	69 -**286**
Ryo Ishikawa	T17	Round 1	4	4	3	4	4	4	4	3	3	4	3	3	5	5	4	4	4	3	68
Japan	T21	Round 2	3	5	4	4	4	5	4	4	3	4	3	4	5	5	4	5	4	3	73
£31,250	T41	Round 3	4	4	4	4	5	5	4	3	4	4	3	4	5	7	4	3	5	3	75
	T27	Round 4	3	3	5	4	4	4	4	3	3	4	3	5	4	5	4	4	5	3	70 -**286**
Bradley Dredge	T3	Round 1	3	4	3	4	4	4	4	3	4	3	4	3	4	4	4	4	4	3	66
Wales	T28	Round 2	4	5	4	4	4	5	4	3	4	4	3	4	3	6	4	4	7	4	76
£31,250	T41	Round 3	5	4	3	4	5	4	3	3	3	6	3	4	4	5	4	4	6	4	74
	T27	Round 4	4	3	3	5	5	4	4	3	4	4	4	4	4	4	4	4	4	3	70 -**286**
Marcel Siem	T8	Round 1	4	3	4	3	4	4	3	3	4	4	4	4	3	6	4	4	4	3	67
Germany	T28	Round 2	3	4	4	4	5	4	4	3	5	4	2	4	4	5	5	4	7	4	75
£31,250	T41	Round 3	4	4	4	4	5	6	3	4	3	4	3	4	5	5	4	4	5	3	74
	T27	Round 4	3	4	4	4	5	4	4	3	3	3	3	4	3	6	4	4	6	3	70 -**286**
Robert Allenby	T30	Round 1	4	3	4	4	4	4	4	3	4	4	3	4	3	5	4	4	4	4	69
Australia	T43	Round 2	5	5	4	4	6	4	4	3	4	4	3	4	4	5	4	4	4	4	75
£31,250	T38	Round 3	4	4	4	4	5	5	4	3	4	3	3	3	4	5	4	4	4	4	71
	T27	Round 4	4	4	4	5	5	3	4	3	3	4	3	4	4	5	4	4	4	4	71 -**286**

HOLE			1	2	3	4	5	6	7	8	9	10	11	12	13	14	15	16	17	18	
PAR	POSITION		4	4	4	4	5	4	4	3	4	4	3	4	4	5	4	4	4	4	TOTAL
Adam Scott	T74	Round 1	4	4	4	4	4	4	4	5	3	4	3	2	5	4	4	5	5	4	72
Australia	T28	Round 2	4	5	3	4	3	4	4	3	3	4	3	4	5	5	4	4	5	3	70
£31,250	T26	Round 3	4	5	5	5	5	4	3	3	4	4	3	4	4	4	3	5	4	3	72
	T27	Round 4	5	4	4	4	4	3	4	3	3	4	4	4	5	4	5	4	4	4	72 -286
Kevin Na	T46	Round 1	4	4	4	4	3	4	4	3	4	4	2	4	4	4	5	5	5	3	70
South Korea	T43	Round 2	4	4	4	5	3	4	3	3	4	4	3	4	4	7	4	6	5	3	74
£31,250	T26	Round 3	4	4	3	4	4	3	4	3	3	4	3	4	5	5	5	5	4	3	70
	T27	Round 4	3	4	4	4	4	4	4	3	4	5	3	5	4	6	4	4	4	3	72 -286
Miguel A Jimenez	T74	Round 1	4	4	4	5	4	5	4	3	3	4	4	3	5	4	4	4	4	4	72
Spain	T7	Round 2	3	3	3	5	4	4	3	3	3	4	4	4	5	5	3	3	4	4	67
£31,250	T18	Round 3	4	5	4	5	4	4	4	2	4	3	3	4	5	5	4	5	6	3	74
	T27	Round 4	4	4	4	4	5	4	4	3	3	4	3	4	5	4	5	4	6	3	73 -286
Alejandro Canizares	T8	Round 1	4	3	4	4	4	5	4	2	3	4	2	4	4	4	4	4	5	3	67
Spain	T3	Round 2	4	4	3	4	4	5	4	3	4	5	3	4	4	5	4	4	4	3	71
£31,250	T4	Round 3	4	4	4	3	5	4	4	3	5	3	3	5	4	4	4	3	5	4	71
	T27	Round 4	4	4	4	6	5	4	4	4	4	4	3	3	5	5	5	4	5	4	77 -286
Vijay Singh	T17	Round 1	4	4	4	5	4	4	3	3	4	4	3	4	3	4	4	4	4	3	68
Fiji	T21	Round 2	4	3	4	4	5	4	4	2	4	4	3	5	5	5	4	5	5	3	73
£22,000	T52	Round 3	4	4	4	6	4	4	3	5	4	5	2	5	5	4	4	5	5	4	76
	T37	Round 4	4	4	4	4	5	3	4	3	4	3	3	4	4	5	4	4	5	3	70 -287
Colm Moriarty	T74	Round 1	4	4	3	4	5	4	4	3	4	3	3	4	4	6	4	5	4	4	72
Republic of Ireland	T56	Round 2	4	4	4	3	5	4	4	3	4	4	2	4	5	5	4	5	5	4	73
£22,000	T52	Round 3	4	4	4	4	4	3	4	3	3	4	3	4	5	6	4	5	5	3	72
	T37	Round 4	4	4	4	4	5	4	4	3	4	3	4	4	4	4	4	4	5	3	70 -287
Hunter Mahan	T30	Round 1	4	4	3	4	5	4	4	3	3	3	3	3	4	4	4	5	5	4	69
USA	T56	Round 2	4	4	4	3	7	4	4	3	4	4	4	4	5	6	4	4	5	3	76
£22,000	T41	Round 3	3	4	4	3	5	4	4	3	4	3	4	4	4	4	4	5	6	3	71
	T37	Round 4	4	4	5	4	4	4	4	3	3	3	3	4	4	6	3	4	5	4	71 -287
Soren Kjeldsen	T74	Round 1	4	4	4	5	5	4	4	3	3	4	3	4	4	5	4	4	4	4	72
Denmark	T68	Round 2	4	5	3	5	4	4	4	3	4	4	4	5	3	5	5	4	5	3	74
£22,000	T41	Round 3	4	4	3	3	5	3	4	3	3	4	3	5	4	5	5	4	5	3	70
	T37	Round 4	4	3	3	4	4	4	5	4	2	4	2	4	4	7	4	4	5	4	71 -287
Peter Hanson	T3	Round 1	4	3	3	4	4	4	4	3	4	3	4	4	4	5	3	4	3	3	66
Sweden	T7	Round 2	4	5	4	4	4	4	3	3	4	4	4	4	3	5	4	5	5	4	73
£22,000	T18	Round 3	4	5	4	4	5	5	3	2	4	4	4	4	5	5	5	4	3	4	74
	T37	Round 4	4	4	4	4	5	3	4	4	4	4	3	4	5	5	4	5	5	3	74 -287
Ross Fisher	T17	Round 1	4	4	4	5	4	4	3	2	3	4	2	4	4	4	5	5	4	3	68
England	T56	Round 2	4	5	4	5	5	4	5	4	4	4	3	5	4	4	5	4	4	4	77
£22,000	T18	Round 3	4	4	4	4	4	4	4	3	4	3	3	3	4	4	3	4	6	3	68
	T37	Round 4	4	4	4	4	5	5	4	3	5	4	3	4	4	5	4	4	4	4	74 -287
Shane Lowry	T17	Round 1	4	5	3	4	4	4	3	3	4	3	3	3	5	5	4	4	4	3	68
Republic of Ireland	T21	Round 2	4	6	4	4	5	4	4	3	3	5	3	4	4	5	4	4	4	3	73
£22,000	T12	Round 3	4	4	4	4	5	4	4	3	4	4	3	3	4	5	4	5	4	3	71
	T37	Round 4	4	3	5	5	5	4	4	3	4	5	2	4	4	5	5	4	6	3	75 -287
Darren Clarke	T46	Round 1	4	5	4	4	4	4	4	2	3	4	3	4	5	4	4	3	5	4	70
Northern Ireland	T14	Round 2	4	4	3	4	6	4	3	3	4	4	3	5	3	4	4	4	5	3	70
£17,125	T52	Round 3	5	4	4	4	4	5	4	3	4	5	3	5	5	5	3	4	7	3	77
	T44	Round 4	3	4	4	4	5	4	3	3	4	5	3	4	4	5	4	4	5	3	71 -288

HOLE			1	2	3	4	5	6	7	8	9	10	11	12	13	14	15	16	17	18	
PAR	POSITION		4	4	4	4	5	4	4	3	4	4	3	4	4	5	4	4	4	4	TOTAL
Bo Van Pelt	T30	Round 1	3	4	4	4	6	4	4	3	3	4	3	5	3	4	3	4	5	3	69
USA	T21	Round 2	4	5	4	5	4	4	4	2	4	4	4	4	4	5	5	3	4	3	72
£17,125	T26	Round 3	4	4	4	4	5	4	4	3	3	4	4	4	5	4	4	4	5	4	73
	T44	Round 4	4	4	4	4	4	4	5	3	4	4	3	5	4	6	4	4	4	4	74 -**288**
Camilo Villegas	T17	Round 1	4	4	3	4	5	4	4	3	3	3	3	3	4	5	4	4	4	4	68
Colombia	T38	Round 2	5	4	4	4	6	5	4	2	5	4	3	4	5	4	4	4	4	4	75
£17,125	T18	Round 3	4	4	4	4	4	6	3	3	4	4	3	3	5	5	4	4	3	3	70
	T44	Round 4	5	4	4	4	5	4	5	3	3	4	3	4	4	5	5	4	5	5	75 -**288**
Ricky Barnes	T17	Round 1	3	4	4	4	4	3	5	3	3	4	3	3	4	5	4	4	4	4	68
USA	T7	Round 2	3	4	4	4	3	4	3	3	4	3	3	4	4	7	5	4	5	4	71
£17,125	T8	Round 3	5	4	3	4	5	3	4	4	3	5	3	4	4	4	4	5	5	3	72
	T44	Round 4	4	4	4	4	5	4	4	4	3	4	3	4	5	7	4	4	6	4	77 -**288**
John Senden	T17	Round 1	4	4	4	4	4	3	4	3	3	4	2	4	4	4	4	4	5	4	68
Australia	T43	Round 2	4	3	4	4	5	6	4	3	4	4	3	4	4	6	6	4	5	3	76
£13,757	T52	Round 3	4	3	4	4	5	4	3	5	4	4	3	4	5	4	4	5	5	3	73
	T48	Round 4	4	4	3	4	5	4	4	3	3	4	3	4	4	6	4	4	5	4	72 -**289**
Simon Dyson	T30	Round 1	4	5	3	4	4	4	3	3	4	4	2	3	4	5	4	5	4	4	69
England	T43	Round 2	4	4	4	4	5	5	4	4	4	5	3	3	4	4	4	5	5	4	75
£13,757	T52	Round 3	4	4	4	5	5	4	4	3	3	4	3	4	4	5	5	5	4	3	73
	T48	Round 4	3	4	4	5	5	4	4	3	4	4	3	4	4	5	4	4	4	4	72 -**289**
Kyung-tae Kim	T46	Round 1	3	4	4	4	4	4	3	3	3	4	3	3	5	5	4	5	5	5	70
South Korea	T43	Round 2	4	4	4	4	4	4	5	3	4	4	3	4	4	5	4	5	5	4	74
£13,757	T52	Round 3	4	4	4	4	5	4	4	3	4	3	2	5	4	5	4	4	7	3	73
	T48	Round 4	4	4	4	4	7	3	4	4	3	4	3	5	5	4	3	4	4	3	72 -**289**
John Daly	T3	Round 1	3	3	4	4	5	3	4	2	3	3	2	4	4	5	4	4	5	4	66
USA	T28	Round 2	4	4	4	4	5	5	5	3	4	4	4	4	5	4	4	4	5	4	76
£13,757	T41	Round 3	4	5	4	5	5	4	5	3	4	3	4	4	5	5	3	4	3	3	74
	T48	Round 4	4	3	4	4	7	4	4	3	4	4	3	6	3	5	4	4	4	4	73 -**289**
Stewart Cink	T46	Round 1	4	4	5	4	4	4	4	2	4	4	3	3	4	5	4	4	4	4	70
USA	T43	Round 2	5	4	4	4	4	4	4	3	4	4	4	5	4	4	4	5	4	4	74
£13,757	T38	Round 3	3	5	4	4	5	4	4	3	4	4	3	4	5	4	5	4	4	2	71
	T48	Round 4	4	5	4	4	5	5	4	3	4	4	3	4	4	5	4	4	4	4	74 -**289**
Phil Mickelson	T97	Round 1	4	4	4	4	5	4	4	3	4	4	3	4	6	5	4	4	4	3	73
USA	T43	Round 2	4	4	3	4	3	5	4	3	3	4	3	5	4	6	4	4	5	3	71
£13,757	T26	Round 3	4	5	3	4	5	3	4	3	3	3	3	4	3	5	4	6	5	3	70
	T48	Round 4	4	4	3	4	4	4	4	3	4	4	3	5	4	6	4	6	5	4	75 -**289**
Lucas Glover	T8	Round 1	4	5	3	4	5	4	3	3	4	3	2	4	3	5	3	4	5	3	67
USA	T43	Round 2	4	4	3	4	6	5	4	3	3	5	4	4	5	4	5	4	5	4	76
£13,757	T18	Round 3	4	4	4	5	4	4	3	3	4	3	3	4	5	4	3	4	5	4	70
	T48	Round 4	4	4	5	5	5	4	4	3	4	5	3	4	4	6	4	5	4	3	76 -**289**
Danny Chia	T30	Round 1	4	3	3	4	4	4	4	3	3	4	4	4	5	4	3	4	5	4	69
Malaysia	T68	Round 2	4	4	5	5	5	5	4	3	4	4	3	4	4	5	4	5	5	3	77
£12,400	T72	Round 3	4	4	4	4	3	4	6	3	4	4	5	5	4	5	4	4	4	3	74
	T55	Round 4	4	3	3	4	5	4	5	3	4	3	4	4	5	4	4	4	4	3	70 -**290**
Simon Khan	T117	Round 1	4	4	4	4	5	4	5	3	4	4	4	5	4	4	4	5	3	4	74
England	T38	Round 2	4	3	4	4	4	4	3	3	4	4	3	4	4	6	4	4	4	3	69
£12,400	T41	Round 3	4	4	4	4	5	4	3	3	4	5	3	5	5	5	3	4	5	3	73
	T55	Round 4	4	4	4	4	5	4	4	3	4	4	3	4	4	6	4	4	5	4	74 -**290**

HOLE			1	2	3	4	5	6	7	8	9	10	11	12	13	14	15	16	17	18	
PAR	POSITION		4	4	4	4	5	4	4	3	4	4	3	4	4	5	4	4	4	4	TOTAL
Zane Scotland	T46	Round 1	3	4	4	4	4	4	4	3	4	4	3	4	4	5	4	4	5	3	70
England	T43	Round 2	4	4	4	4	4	6	4	3	3	4	3	5	4	5	4	4	6	3	74
£12,400	T41	Round 3	4	4	4	4	5	3	3	3	4	4	4	4	4	4	5	5	5	3	72
	T55	Round 4	3	5	4	5	5	4	4	3	4	4	3	5	4	5	4	4	5	3	74 -**290**
Steve Stricker	T59	Round 1	4	4	4	4	5	4	3	3	4	4	3	4	4	6	4	4	4	3	71
USA	T56	Round 2	3	6	4	5	5	3	4	4	4	4	3	4	4	4	4	4	5	4	74
£12,400	T41	Round 3	5	4	4	6	4	3	3	3	4	4	3	3	5	4	4	4	5	3	71
	T55	Round 4	4	4	4	4	5	4	4	3	3	4	3	4	5	5	3	7	4	4	74 -**290**
Steve Marino	T30	Round 1	4	4	4	4	5	4	4	3	3	3	3	3	4	5	4	4	4	4	69
USA	T56	Round 2	4	5	4	5	5	4	4	4	4	4	3	4	6	4	4	5	4	3	76
£12,400	T26	Round 3	4	3	4	4	4	4	4	3	4	4	3	4	4	4	4	4	5	3	69
	T55	Round 4	4	4	3	4	5	4	4	6	4	5	3	4	4	4	4	6	4	4	76 -**290**
Ian Poulter	T59	Round 1	4	4	3	4	5	4	4	3	3	4	3	5	4	5	3	4	5	4	71
England	T43	Round 2	4	4	4	3	5	4	4	3	4	5	4	4	4	4	4	4	5	4	73
£11,750	T72	Round 3	5	4	4	4	5	4	6	3	4	4	3	4	4	5	4	5	4	4	76
	T60	Round 4	4	4	3	5	4	3	3	3	3	4	3	4	3	6	4	5	6	4	71 -**291**
Jason Day	T59	Round 1	4	5	4	4	5	3	4	4	3	4	3	3	3	5	4	5	4	4	71
Australia	T56	Round 2	4	4	4	4	6	4	5	3	4	4	4	4	4	4	4	4	4	4	74
£11,750	T72	Round 3	4	6	3	4	7	4	4	3	4	5	3	4	5	4	4	4	4	3	75
	T60	Round 4	3	4	4	6	4	4	4	3	4	4	3	4	5	4	4	4	3	3	71 -**291**
Peter Senior	T97	Round 1	4	4	5	4	4	4	4	3	4	3	4	3	4	6	4	5	5	3	73
Australia	T43	Round 2	3	5	3	4	5	4	4	3	4	4	3	4	4	5	5	4	4	3	71
£11,750	T65	Round 3	4	5	4	4	4	4	5	3	4	4	3	4	4	6	4	4	4	4	74
	T60	Round 4	3	5	4	4	4	4	4	3	4	3	4	4	5	5	4	4	5	4	73 -**291**
Heath Slocum	T59	Round 1	4	3	4	4	4	4	4	3	4	4	3	4	4	4	4	4	6	4	71
USA	T56	Round 2	3	5	4	4	5	4	3	3	4	4	4	5	4	5	4	4	5	4	74
£11,750	T65	Round 3	4	5	4	4	5	4	3	3	4	4	3	4	4	5	5	4	5	3	73
	T60	Round 4	4	3	4	4	4	4	4	3	3	5	3	4	5	5	4	4	6	4	73 -**291**
Toru Taniguchi	T46	Round 1	4	4	4	4	3	3	4	3	4	4	3	4	4	4	5	4	5	4	70
Japan	T14	Round 2	3	4	4	4	5	4	4	3	4	4	3	4	4	5	4	4	4	3	70
£11,750	T52	Round 3	6	4	3	5	7	3	4	4	4	4	3	4	4	5	4	4	5	4	77
	T60	Round 4	5	6	4	4	5	4	3	3	3	4	3	5	4	5	4	4	4	3	74 -**291**
YE Yang	T8	Round 1	3	4	4	4	4	4	4	3	4	4	3	3	4	4	4	4	4	3	67
South Korea	T21	Round 2	4	4	4	4	4	5	5	3	4	4	5	4	4	4	4	4	4	4	74
£11,750	T52	Round 3	5	3	5	5	6	4	4	3	3	5	3	4	4	5	4	4	6	3	76
	T60	Round 4	3	6	4	4	4	4	4	2	5	4	2	4	5	4	4	7	5	3	74 -**291**
Tom Pernice Jr	T74	Round 1	6	3	4	4	4	4	4	3	4	3	3	4	5	6	4	4	3	4	72
USA	T68	Round 2	4	4	5	4	4	5	5	3	4	4	3	4	4	4	4	4	6	3	74
£11,750	T52	Round 3	3	4	4	4	5	4	4	3	4	4	3	4	4	4	4	5	5	4	71
	T60	Round 4	4	5	4	5	5	3	3	3	4	4	3	4	4	5	6	4	4	4	74 -**291**
Marc Leishman	T97	Round 1	4	4	4	3	5	4	4	2	3	4	4	5	5	5	4	4	5	4	73
Australia	T43	Round 2	3	5	4	4	5	4	3	3	4	4	2	3	4	5	4	6	4	4	71
£11,750	T41	Round 3	4	4	3	4	6	4	4	4	4	4	3	4	4	5	4	4	4	3	72
	T60	Round 4	3	4	4	5	5	5	4	3	3	4	4	4	5	5	4	4	5	4	75 -**291**
Colin Montgomerie	T117	Round 1	4	4	4	5	4	4	4	3	4	3	3	3	4	5	5	4	6	4	74
Scotland	T56	Round 2	4	4	4	4	5	4	4	3	3	4	3	5	4	5	3	4	4	4	71
£11,150	T69	Round 3	4	5	6	5	3	4	4	3	3	4	3	4	5	4	4	4	6	3	74
	T68	Round 4	4	4	4	5	4	4	3	3	4	4	3	4	4	5	4	4	6	4	73 -**292**

HOLE			1	2	3	4	5	6	7	8	9	10	11	12	13	14	15	16	17	18	
PAR	POSITION		4	4	4	4	5	4	4	3	4	4	3	4	4	5	4	4	4	4	TOTAL
Hirofumi Miyase	T59	Round 1	4	4	4	3	4	4	4	4	3	4	3	4	5	6	3	4	4	4	71
Japan	T68	Round 2	4	5	4	4	5	5	3	3	4	4	3	4	4	5	4	5	5	4	75
£11,150	T69	Round 3	4	4	4	4	5	4	4	3	4	4	4	4	4	5	4	4	4	4	73
	T68	Round 4	4	4	3	4	4	4	4	3	4	3	4	5	4	6	4	5	5	3	73 **-292**
Steven Tiley	T3	Round 1	3	4	4	4	4	3	4	3	3	4	3	4	3	5	3	4	4	4	66
England	T56	Round 2	4	4	4	5	4	4	4	3	4	4	5	5	4	6	5	5	5	4	79
£11,150	T65	Round 3	4	3	4	5	4	4	4	3	4	4	3	4	6	5	4	5	3	4	73
	T68	Round 4	4	4	4	5	5	4	4	2	4	4	3	4	4	5	4	4	5	5	74 **-292**
Fredrick	T8	Round 1	3	4	4	3	4	3	4	3	4	4	3	4	3	4	5	4	5	3	67
Andersson Hed	T21	Round 2	4	5	3	4	4	5	4	4	4	4	3	5	4	5	4	4	4	4	74
Sweden	T26	Round 3	4	4	4	4	4	5	4	4	3	4	3	5	4	6	4	3	4	4	73
£11,150	**T68**	Round 4	4	4	4	4	7	5	2	3	3	3	3	5	5	7	5	5	6	3	78 **-292**
Andrew Coltart	T3	Round 1	4	4	4	4	4	3	4	3	3	3	4	4	4	4	3	4	4	3	66
Scotland	T38	Round 2	5	4	4	4	5	5	4	4	4	3	4	4	5	6	4	4	5	3	77
£10,900	T52	Round 3	5	3	4	4	4	5	5	3	3	4	3	4	5	4	5	3	6	4	74
	72	Round 4	4	4	5	4	5	4	3	3	4	5	3	4	4	6	4	4	6	4	76 **-293**
Mark Calcavecchia	T46	Round 1	5	4	4	3	6	4	4	3	4	4	3	4	3	4	3	4	5	3	70
USA	2	Round 2	4	4	4	3	4	4	4	3	4	4	2	3	4	5	4	4	4	3	67
£10,800	T26	Round 3	5	5	5	4	9	4	4	3	4	4	3	3	3	4	4	4	5	4	77
	73	Round 4	5	4	5	5	5	4	4	3	3	3	4	4	5	5	4	7	6	4	80 **-294**
Richard S Johnson	T97	Round 1	5	4	4	4	5	3	4	3	4	4	4	4	4	5	4	5	4	4	73
Sweden	T68	Round 2	4	4	4	4	5	4	3	3	4	3	3	5	6	5	5	4	4	3	73
£10,650	77	Round 3	4	4	3	4	5	4	5	3	4	4	3	5	4	6	4	5	5	4	76
	T74	Round 4	4	4	4	4	4	3	5	3	3	3	5	4	4	5	4	5	5	4	73 **-295**
Thomas Aiken	T59	Round 1	3	5	5	4	4	4	4	3	4	4	3	4	4	4	4	4	4	4	71
South Africa	T43	Round 2	4	4	4	5	4	5	4	3	3	4	4	4	4	5	5	5	4	3	73
£10,650	76	Round 3	5	4	3	4	5	4	4	3	4	4	4	4	5	5	4	5	4	6	77
	T74	Round 4	4	4	5	4	4	4	4	3	4	5	3	4	5	5	4	4	5	3	74 **-295**
Zach Johnson	T74	Round 1	3	4	3	4	5	4	3	3	4	4	3	5	5	5	4	4	5	4	72
USA	T68	Round 2	4	5	3	4	5	5	4	3	4	4	3	5	4	5	4	3	5	4	74
£10,450	T72	Round 3	4	3	3	5	5	4	4	3	4	4	3	4	4	6	4	4	6	4	74
	T76	Round 4	3	4	4	4	6	3	5	3	4	4	4	4	4	6	4	4	5	5	76 **-296**
Scott Verplank	T74	Round 1	3	5	4	4	4	5	4	3	4	4	3	5	4	4	4	4	4	4	72
USA	T56	Round 2	3	4	4	3	5	4	4	3	4	4	3	4	4	5	4	4	7	4	73
£10,450	T69	Round 3	4	4	4	5	5	3	5	3	4	5	3	4	4	5	5	4	3	4	74
	T76	Round 4	4	4	4	5	5	4	4	3	4	5	3	5	5	5	6	4	4	3	77 **-296**

NON QUALIFIERS AFTER 36 HOLES

(Leading 10 professionals and ties receive £3,400 each, next 20 professionals and ties receive £2,750 each, next 20 professionals and ties receive £2,500 each, remainder of professionals receive £2,250 each.)

HOLE			1	2	3	4	5	6	7	8	9	10	11	12	13	14	15	16	17	18	
PAR	POSITION		4	4	4	4	5	4	4	3	4	4	3	4	4	5	4	4	4	4	TOTAL
Eric Chun*	T59	Round 1	3	5	3	4	4	4	4	3	4	4	3	4	4	5	4	5	4	4	71
South Korea	**T78**	Round 2	4	4	4	4	5	4	4	3	4	4	3	4	5	5	4	5	6	4	76-147
Bubba Watson	T117	Round 1	4	4	4	4	5	4	5	3	4	4	4	4	3	6	5	3	5	3	74
USA	**T78**	Round 2	4	4	4	4	4	3	4	3	4	4	4	4	5	4	5	4	5	4	73-147
Oliver Wilson	T17	Round 1	5	4	3	4	4	3	4	2	3	4	3	4	4	5	3	4	5	4	68
England	**T78**	Round 2	4	5	5	6	5	4	4	2	4	4	4	4	5	5	5	4	5	4	79-147
Thomas Bjorn	T46	Round 1	3	5	4	4	6	4	4	3	4	3	3	4	4	4	3	4	4	4	70
Denmark	**T78**	Round 2	4	4	5	4	5	4	5	3	5	4	4	4	4	5	5	4	4	4	77-147
Justin Rose	T46	Round 1	3	3	4	4	5	4	4	4	4	4	3	3	4	4	4	4	5	4	70
England	**T78**	Round 2	5	4	4	4	4	5	4	3	4	4	5	4	5	4	6	4	4	4	77-147
Mark O'Meara	T30	Round 1	3	3	4	4	5	5	3	3	3	4	3	4	4	4	4	4	5	4	69
USA	**T78**	Round 2	5	6	4	5	6	4	4	3	4	3	3	4	4	5	5	4	5	4	78-147
Gregory Havret	T97	Round 1	3	5	4	5	4	4	4	3	3	4	3	5	3	6	4	4	5	4	73
France	**T78**	Round 2	4	5	4	4	4	4	4	3	4	4	4	4	5	6	4	4	4	4	74-147
Tom Whitehouse	T97	Round 1	4	4	4	4	4	5	3	3	4	4	3	4	4	6	5	4	5	3	73
England	**T78**	Round 2	4	5	4	4	5	4	4	3	4	4	4	5	4	5	4	4	3	4	74-147
Rhys Davies	T97	Round 1	4	4	4	5	4	4	4	3	4	3	3	4	4	5	4	4	5	4	73
Wales	**T86**	Round 2	5	7	4	5	5	3	3	3	3	4	4	4	4	4	5	5	4	4	75-148
Ben Crane	T74	Round 1	4	4	4	4	4	4	4	3	4	4	4	4	4	4	4	4	6	5	72
USA	**T86**	Round 2	3	4	4	4	4	4	3	4	4	4	5	6	6	5	4	5	4	3	76-148
Gareth Maybin	T74	Round 1	4	5	4	4	4	4	4	3	4	4	3	4	4	5	3	4	5	4	72
Northern Ireland	**T86**	Round 2	4	3	4	5	4	4	4	3	4	5	4	5	5	5	4	5	4	4	76-148
Ryuichi Oda	T134	Round 1	4	4	3	4	5	5	3	3	4	4	3	4	4	6	4	6	5	5	76
Japan	**T86**	Round 2	4	5	3	3	5	4	4	3	3	4	3	5	5	5	4	4	5	3	72-148
Seung-Yul Noh	T74	Round 1	4	5	4	4	4	4	4	3	3	4	3	4	4	4	4	6	4	4	72
South Korea	**T86**	Round 2	4	4	4	4	5	5	4	4	4	6	3	4	5	5	4	4	4	3	76-148
Ross McGowan	T17	Round 1	4	3	4	4	3	4	4	3	3	4	4	3	5	4	4	5	4	3	68
England	**T86**	Round 2	4	4	5	6	5	4	3	5	3	4	5	5	5	5	4	4	4	4	80-148
G Fernandez-Castano	T74	Round 1	4	5	4	4	5	4	3	3	3	4	3	4	4	4	4	4	6	4	72
Spain	**T86**	Round 2	4	5	4	5	5	4	5	3	4	4	3	3	5	4	5	5	5	3	76-148
Ernie Els	T30	Round 1	4	4	4	4	5	4	4	3	3	4	3	4	4	5	4	3	4	3	69
South Africa	**T86**	Round 2	4	5	5	4	5	4	5	3	5	4	4	4	4	5	4	5	5	4	79-148
Tom Watson	T97	Round 1	4	5	5	5	4	4	4	3	4	4	4	4	4	4	4	4	4	4	73
USA	**T86**	Round 2	4	4	4	4	7	4	4	4	3	4	3	4	4	5	4	5	5	3	75-148
Mike Weir	T97	Round 1	4	5	4	4	4	3	3	3	4	4	3	4	4	4	5	5	6	4	73
Canada	**T86**	Round 2	4	4	4	5	5	5	4	4	3	4	5	4	4	4	4	4	4	3	75-148
Tano Goya	T46	Round 1	5	4	4	5	4	4	4	3	3	4	3	3	4	5	4	4	3	4	70
Argentina	**T86**	Round 2	4	5	4	4	5	4	4	4	4	4	3	4	5	5	5	4	6	4	78-148
Ben Curtis	T134	Round 1	4	4	4	5	5	3	4	3	4	4	4	4	4	6	5	4	6	3	76
USA	**T97**	Round 2	4	4	4	5	5	4	4	2	4	6	4	4	5	4	3	4	3	3	73-149
Angel Cabrera	T97	Round 1	4	5	4	4	5	4	4	3	4	3	3	4	6	4	4	4	4	4	73
Argentina	**T97**	Round 2	5	4	4	4	5	4	4	3	4	4	4	5	5	4	4	4	5	4	76-149
Jason Bohn	T127	Round 1	4	4	4	5	4	6	4	3	3	4	3	4	4	5	5	5	4	4	75
USA	**T97**	Round 2	4	5	3	4	5	4	3	4	3	4	3	4	4	5	4	4	7	4	74-149
DA Points	T74	Round 1	4	5	4	5	5	3	4	3	4	2	4	6	4	4	4	4	4	4	72
USA	**T97**	Round 2	5	4	4	4	5	4	3	3	3	5	4	5	5	5	4	4	5	5	77-149

HOLE			1	2	3	4	5	6	7	8	9	10	11	12	13	14	15	16	17	18	
PAR	POSITION		4	4	4	4	5	4	4	3	4	4	3	4	4	5	4	4	4	4	TOTAL
Todd Hamilton	T74	Round 1	4	4	4	4	5	4	3	3	4	4	4	4	4	5	4	4	4	4	72
USA	**T97**	Round 2	4	4	4	4	5	4	4	3	4	5	4	5	5	6	4	5	4	3	77-**149**
Chris Wood	T46	Round 1	3	5	4	4	4	4	3	3	4	4	3	3	4	5	5	4	5	3	70
England	**T97**	Round 2	5	3	5	5	5	4	5	3	4	5	4	4	6	4	5	4	4	4	79-**149**
Davis Love III	T97	Round 1	4	4	4	4	5	4	4	4	4	3	3	5	4	4	4	4	6	3	73
USA	**T97**	Round 2	5	5	4	4	5	4	4	3	4	4	3	4	6	5	4	5	4	3	76-**149**
Michael Sim	T74	Round 1	4	5	4	5	4	5	3	3	4	4	3	3	4	5	3	4	5	4	72
Australia	**T97**	Round 2	4	4	4	5	4	4	4	4	4	4	3	5	4	6	5	4	5	4	77-**149**
Koumei Oda	T117	Round 1	5	4	4	4	5	3	4	3	3	5	3	4	4	5	5	5	5	3	74
Japan	**T105**	Round 2	4	5	4	4	5	4	4	3	4	4	4	5	4	5	4	4	5	4	76-**150**
Jim Furyk	T142	Round 1	4	4	4	4	6	4	5	4	3	4	4	5	5	5	4	5	4	3	77
USA	**T105**	Round 2	3	4	4	5	4	5	4	4	4	4	3	3	5	4	5	4	4	4	73-**150**
Geoff Ogilvy	T74	Round 1	4	4	4	5	5	4	3	3	5	3	3	4	4	4	5	4	4	4	72
Australia	**T105**	Round 2	4	4	4	5	6	3	4	3	5	4	3	4	5	4	5	5	6	4	78-**150**
Hiroyuki Fujita	T127	Round 1	3	4	4	5	6	5	4	3	4	4	3	4	4	5	4	4	5	3	75
Japan	**T105**	Round 2	4	4	4	4	5	4	4	3	4	4	3	3	4	5	5	4	7	4	75-**150**
Justin Leonard	T134	Round 1	4	6	3	4	6	5	4	3	4	3	3	4	5	5	4	4	5	4	76
USA	**T105**	Round 2	3	4	5	4	5	5	4	3	4	4	4	3	5	5	4	4	5	3	74-**150**
KJ Choi	T134	Round 1	4	5	4	6	4	4	4	3	4	5	3	4	4	5	4	5	4	4	76
South Korea	**T105**	Round 2	4	4	3	4	4	5	5	3	4	4	4	4	6	4	5	4	4	4	74-**150**
Paul Goydos	T117	Round 1	4	5	5	4	4	4	3	3	4	4	4	4	4	5	5	4	4	4	74
USA	**T105**	Round 2	3	4	4	5	4	5	4	3	5	5	4	4	5	5	4	4	4	4	76-**150**
Bill Haas	T97	Round 1	4	3	4	4	5	4	4	3	4	4	3	4	4	5	4	5	5	4	73
USA	**T105**	Round 2	4	4	4	5	5	5	4	3	4	3	4	5	4	5	5	5	6	3	77-**150**
Yuka Ikeda	T74	Round 1	3	4	4	4	4	4	4	3	4	4	3	4	6	4	4	4	5	4	72
Japan	**T105**	Round 2	5	4	4	5	4	4	5	3	4	5	4	4	5	5	5	5	4	3	78-**150**
Padraig Harrington	T97	Round 1	6	3	5	4	4	4	4	3	4	4	3	4	4	4	3	5	5	4	73
Republic of Ireland	**T105**	Round 2	5	6	4	4	5	4	5	3	4	4	3	4	4	5	5	4	5	3	77-**150**
Kenny Perry	T59	Round 1	3	5	4	4	5	3	4	3	4	4	3	4	4	4	5	4	5	3	71
USA	**T105**	Round 2	4	4	4	5	5	5	5	3	6	5	3	4	5	5	4	5	4	5	79-**150**
Anders Hansen	T142	Round 1	4	5	4	4	6	4	4	3	3	4	4	4	4	6	4	4	8	2	77
Denmark	**T116**	Round 2	4	3	4	4	5	4	4	3	4	4	3	5	5	5	4	5	4	4	74-**151**
Sandy Lyle	T127	Round 1	4	5	4	5	4	4	4	3	4	4	3	3	4	4	5	4	7	4	75
Scotland	**T116**	Round 2	4	5	5	5	4	4	4	3	4	4	3	4	5	5	4	4	5	4	76-**151**
Francesco Molinari	T117	Round 1	4	4	4	4	6	4	4	4	5	4	3	4	4	4	4	5	4	4	74
Italy	**T116**	Round 2	4	5	4	4	5	4	4	3	4	4	3	4	5	5	5	4	7	3	77-**151**
Tim Petrovic	T59	Round 1	4	5	4	4	4	4	4	3	3	4	4	3	5	5	4	4	4	3	71
USA	**T116**	Round 2	3	4	4	5	5	5	5	4	3	5	5	4	6	5	4	5	5	3	80-**151**
Jean Hugo	T134	Round 1	4	5	3	5	4	4	4	4	4	4	4	3	5	7	4	4	4	4	76
South Africa	**T116**	Round 2	4	5	4	5	5	4	3	3	3	4	3	5	5	4	4	5	5	4	75-**151**
Paul Lawrie	T30	Round 1	4	3	4	5	5	4	4	4	3	4	3	4	4	4	4	3	4	3	69
Scotland	**T116**	Round 2	4	4	5	5	5	4	5	4	4	4	4	4	5	7	4	5	5	4	82-**151**
Loren Roberts	T97	Round 1	4	3	3	4	5	3	4	4	4	4	4	4	5	5	5	4	4	4	73
USA	**T116**	Round 2	5	4	4	4	5	4	4	3	4	5	3	4	6	6	3	5	6	3	78-**151**
Soren Hansen	T74	Round 1	5	4	4	4	4	4	5	3	4	4	3	4	4	4	4	4	4	4	72
Denmark	**T116**	Round 2	5	4	4	4	5	4	5	4	4	6	5	4	4	5	3	5	4	4	79-**151**
Tim Clark	T59	Round 1	5	3	4	5	5	4	5	3	3	3	3	4	3	5	4	4	4	4	71
South Africa	**T116**	Round 2	3	5	4	5	6	3	4	4	5	4	4	5	6	7	4	4	4	3	80-**151**
Byeong-Hun An*	T74	Round 1	4	4	3	4	4	4	6	3	3	4	3	4	6	4	4	5	4	3	72
South Korea	**T116**	Round 2	4	5	4	4	6	5	4	4	6	4	4	5	5	5	4	3	4	3	79-**151**

HOLE			1	2	3	4	5	6	7	8	9	10	11	12	13	14	15	16	17	18	
PAR	POSITION		4	4	4	4	5	4	4	3	4	4	3	4	4	5	4	4	4	4	TOTAL
Phillip Archer	T127	Round 1	3	4	5	4	4	4	4	3	4	4	3	4	4	6	4	4	7	4	75
England	**T116**	Round 2	4	4	3	5	5	3	4	4	5	4	3	4	5	5	5	4	5	4	76-151
Kurt Barnes	T127	Round 1	5	4	4	4	5	6	4	2	4	4	4	4	4	4	4	4	5	4	75
Australia	**T127**	Round 2	4	5	4	5	5	4	4	4	4	5	3	5	4	4	4	4	5	4	77-152
Darren Fichardt	T117	Round 1	4	3	4	6	5	5	4	3	4	4	3	4	4	4	4	4	5	4	74
South Africa	**T127**	Round 2	5	4	4	4	5	4	5	3	5	5	3	5	5	5	3	4	5	4	78-152
Paul Streeter	T134	Round 1	4	4	4	4	3	3	5	4	4	4	3	5	5	5	5	5	5	4	76
England	**T127**	Round 2	4	4	4	4	5	5	4	4	3	5	3	5	4	5	4	4	4	4	76-152
Josh Cunliffe	T127	Round 1	3	5	3	4	4	4	5	4	4	4	3	5	5	6	5	3	4	4	75
South Africa	**T127**	Round 2	4	4	4	5	5	4	6	3	4	3	3	5	5	5	4	5	4	4	77-152
Shunsuke Sonoda	T117	Round 1	5	4	4	5	5	4	4	3	4	4	3	4	4	5	4	4	4	4	74
Japan	**T127**	Round 2	4	5	4	4	5	4	4	4	4	5	4	4	4	5	5	4	4	5	78-152
Thongchai Jaidee	T127	Round 1	4	5	4	4	5	5	4	3	3	4	3	4	4	4	5	4	4	4	75
Thailand	**T127**	Round 2	5	4	4	5	4	4	3	4	4	5	4	5	4	4	4	4	6	4	77-152
Jamie Abbott*	T97	Round 1	3	4	4	5	5	4	3	4	4	4	3	4	4	5	3	4	6	4	73
England	**T127**	Round 2	5	5	4	5	5	5	4	4	4	4	4	5	4	4	4	4	4	4	79-152
Katsumasa Miyamoto	T142	Round 1	4	5	4	4	5	4	4	3	4	4	3	7	5	5	3	6	4	3	77
Japan	**T134**	Round 2	3	3	4	5	5	5	4	3	4	4	3	4	4	5	5	4	4	7	76-153
Victor Dubuisson*	T153	Round 1	4	6	4	4	4	4	5	4	4	6	3	4	4	4	4	4	6	6	80
France	**T134**	Round 2	4	4	4	4	5	4	4	2	4	4	4	4	5	5	4	4	4	4	73-153
Mathew Goggin	T117	Round 1	4	4	3	4	5	4	4	3	4	4	3	4	4	5	4	5	6	4	74
Australia	**T134**	Round 2	5	4	4	4	5	4	4	3	4	4	4	5	5	5	4	5	6	4	79-153
Alexander Noren	T97	Round 1	4	4	4	4	4	4	4	3	4	4	3	4	5	6	4	4	4	4	73
Sweden	**T134**	Round 2	5	5	4	4	5	5	4	3	5	5	3	5	5	5	5	4	4	4	80-153
Sir Nick Faldo	T74	Round 1	4	5	4	4	4	4	4	3	4	4	3	4	4	5	4	4	5	3	72
England	**T134**	Round 2	4	5	5	6	5	4	4	4	4	4	3	5	5	5	6	3	5	4	81-153
Jerry Kelly	T149	Round 1	4	5	5	4	4	7	4	3	4	4	4	4	5	5	4	4	5	4	79
USA	**T139**	Round 2	4	4	4	5	4	3	4	3	3	4	3	6	5	4	5	5	5	4	75-154
Thomas Levet	T97	Round 1	4	3	4	4	4	4	3	4	4	3	4	5	4	4	5	5	4	4	73
France	**T139**	Round 2	4	4	4	6	5	4	5	3	4	6	3	6	5	6	4	4	4	4	81-154
Ryan Moore	T46	Round 1	3	4	5	5	4	3	4	3	4	3	3	4	3	5	4	5	4	4	70
USA	**T139**	Round 2	4	5	4	4	5	3	5	3	5	6	5	4	7	5	4	4	8	3	84-154
Mark F Haastrup	T74	Round 1	4	4	4	4	5	4	3	3	3	4	3	4	4	5	4	5	4	5	72
Denmark	**T139**	Round 2	4	5	4	5	7	5	4	3	3	4	3	4	4	9	4	4	4	6	82-154
Jose Manuel Lara	T153	Round 1	4	5	4	6	5	4	4	4	4	4	4	4	5	4	5	6	4	4	80
Spain	**T143**	Round 2	4	4	4	5	5	6	4	3	4	4	3	4	4	5	3	5	4	4	75-155
Brian Gay	T74	Round 1	3	4	3	5	4	5	4	3	4	4	4	4	3	6	4	4	4	4	72
USA	**T143**	Round 2	4	4	5	5	4	4	4	4	5	5	4	4	6	5	5	5	7	3	83-155
Tyrrell Hatton*	T146	Round 1	4	5	4	5	4	6	5	3	4	4	3	5	4	6	4	3	4	5	78
England	**T143**	Round 2	4	4	3	5	5	4	3	3	4	4	5	4	5	5	4	5	6	4	77-155
Jae-Bum Park	T134	Round 1	4	4	4	4	4	5	3	4	4	4	4	5	5	4	5	5	4	4	76
South Korea	**T143**	Round 2	3	4	4	5	5	4	5	4	4	5	3	5	6	5	4	4	5	4	79-155
George McNeill	T146	Round 1	6	5	4	4	5	4	4	3	4	3	3	4	5	5	5	4	5	4	78
USA	**T143**	Round 2	4	4	4	4	5	4	5	4	5	4	3	4	3	5	3	4	6	4	77-155
Jason Dufner	T97	Round 1	4	4	4	5	5	4	3	3	4	4	3	4	4	4	5	4	4	5	73
USA	**T143**	Round 2	4	4	3	5	6	6	5	3	5	5	4	5	5	4	4	4	5	5	82-155
David Duval	T142	Round 1	5	5	4	5	5	3	4	3	4	4	3	4	5	4	4	6	4	4	77
USA	**T143**	Round 2	4	5	3	5	4	5	5	3	4	4	4	4	4	5	4	5	6	4	78-155
Cameron Percy	T134	Round 1	4	4	4	3	5	4	4	4	3	5	4	4	5	5	4	5	5	4	76
Australia	**T143**	Round 2	4	4	4	5	4	6	5	3	5	4	3	3	4	6	4	5	5	5	79-155

HOLE			1	2	3	4	5	6	7	8	9	10	11	12	13	14	15	16	17	18	
PAR	POSITION		4	4	4	4	5	4	4	3	4	4	3	4	4	5	4	4	4	4	TOTAL
Gary Clark	T149	Round 1	4	5	4	6	5	4	5	3	3	4	4	4	5	5	5	4	5	4	79
England	**151**	Round 2	4	5	4	5	5	4	4	2	4	5	3	6	4	7	4	4	4	3	77 -**156**
Glen Day	T146	Round 1	4	4	4	4	5	5	4	4	3	5	4	4	4	6	4	5	6	3	78
USA	**T152**	Round 2	4	5	4	5	5	4	5	4	4	4	3	4	7	5	4	5	4	3	79 -**157**
Martin Laird	T117	Round 1	4	4	4	5	4	4	4	3	4	5	3	3	4	5	5	4	4	5	74
Scotland	**T152**	Round 2	4	5	4	4	5	5	5	7	4	6	3	5	4	5	6	4	4	3	83 -**157**
Ewan Porter	T155	Round 1	4	8	4	4	5	4	4	3	5	6	3	4	5	5	5	4	5	3	81
Australia	**154**	Round 2	4	6	4	4	5	4	4	4	4	4	3	4	6	6	4	4	4	4	78 -**159**
Laurie Canter*	T155	Round 1	5	4	4	6	5	4	4	5	4	6	3	4	4	5	4	4	6	4	81
England	**155**	Round 2	4	4	3	6	5	5	3	4	4	5	4	4	4	4	5	5	6	4	79 -**160**
Simon Edwards	T149	Round 1	4	5	4	6	4	4	4	3	4	4	4	5	4	6	5	4	5	4	79
Wales	**156**	Round 2	5	4	5	5	5	5	5	4	4	6	4	5	5	7	4	3	5	5	86 -**165**

THE TOP TENS

Eagles/Birdies

1. *Louis Oosthuizen* 1/20
2. Graeme McDowell 0/20
3. Miguel Angel Jimenez 0/19
3. Rory McIlroy 1/18
5. Paul Casey 0/18
5. Sean O'Hair 0/18
7. Martin Kaymer 0/17
7. Trevor Immelman 0/17
7. Tiger Woods 0/17
7. Marcel Siem 0/17

Pars

1. Robert Allenby 60
2. Stewart Cink 54
3. Henrik Stenson 53
3. Tom Lehman 53
3. Toru Taniguchi 53
6. Retief Goosen 52
6. Jay Overton 52
6. Steve Marino 52
6. Simon Khan 52
10. 6 players tied 51
Louis Oosthuizen 45

Bogeys

1. Lucas Glover 17
1. Simon Edwards 17
3. Andrew Coltart 16
4. Fredrik Andersson Hed 15
4. Thomas Aiken 15
4. Zach Johnson 15
7. 5 players tied 14
Louis Oosthuizen 6

Double Bogeys/Worse

1. Laurie Canter 6/0
2. Colin Montgomerie 4/0
2. Victor Dubuisson 4/0
2. Ben Crane 4/0
2. YE Yang 3/1
2. Ewan Porter 3/1
7. 10 players tied 3/0
7. 4 players tied 2/1
7. Mark Calcavecchia 1/2
Louis Oosthuizen 0/0

Driving Distance

1. Alvaro Quiros 331.0
2. Dustin Johnson 327.5
3. Ross Fisher 325.4
4. *Louis Oosthuizen* 319.4
5. Thomas Aiken 318.9
6. Jason Day 318.5
6. Jeff Overton 318.5
8. John Daly 318.4
9. Camilo Villegas 318.3
10. Tiger Woods 318.1

Fairways Hit

Maximum of 64

1. *Louis Oosthuizen* 55
2. Nick Watney 53
2. John Senden 53
2. Sergio Garcia 53
2. Richard S Johnson 53
6. Henrik Stenson 52
7. 7 players tied 51

Greens in Regulation

Maximum of 72

1. Edoardo Molinari 62
2. Rory McIlroy 61
2. Paul Casey 61
2. JB Holmes 61
2. Graeme McDowell 61
2. Ross Fisher 61
2. John Senden 61
8. *Louis Oosthuizen* 60
8. Alvaro Quiros 60
8. Rickie Fowler 60
8. Simon Dyson 60
8. Peter Senior 60

Putts

1. Alejandro Canizares 120
1. Ricky Barnes 120
3. *Louis Oosthuizen* 121
3. Henrik Stenson 121
3. Sean O'Hair 121
3. Steve Stricker 121
7. Lee Westwood 122
7. Robert Rock 122
7. Luke Donald 122
10. 7 players tied 124

Statistical Rankings

	Driving Distance	Rank	Fairways Hit	Rank	Greens In Regulation	Rank	Putts	Rank
Thomas Aiken	318.9	5	50	14	52	65	129	47
Robert Allenby	303.0	51	45	55	59	13	131	59
Fredrik Andersson Hed	316.8	13	47	38	49	73	127	30
Ricky Barnes	300.9	55	39	71	52	65	120	1
Mark Calcavecchia	299.1	61	48	29	52	65	124	10
Alejandro Canizares	289.9	73	47	38	49	73	120	1
Paul Casey	313.6	17	51	7	61	2	128	39
Danny Chia	304.4	45	42	65	51	70	128	39
Stewart Cink	307.9	33	49	24	55	39	129	47
Darren Clarke	306.1	40	39	71	53	53	124	10
Andrew Coltart	299.4	60	43	60	53	53	128	39
John Daly	318.4	8	36	76	55	39	128	39
Jason Day	318.5	6	43	60	53	53	125	16
Luke Donald	302.5	53	46	46	54	45	122	7
Bradley Dredge	308.0	32	49	24	56	32	127	30
Simon Dyson	283.5	77	48	29	60	8	134	73
Ross Fisher	325.4	3	46	46	61	2	138	77
Rickie Fowler	309.9	26	50	14	60	8	125	16
Stephen Gallacher	307.8	35	51	7	57	25	126	26
Sergio Garcia	308.1	31	53	2	56	32	128	39
Ignacio Garrido	298.9	62	43	60	56	32	125	16
Lucas Glover	306.6	38	41	66	53	53	129	47
Retief Goosen	300.4	56	46	46	58	18	124	10
Peter Hanson	315.4	14	51	7	57	25	133	69
JB Holmes	315.3	15	48	29	61	2	128	39
Trevor Immelman	314.4	16	47	38	59	13	133	69
Ryo Ishikawa	305.1	41	51	7	55	39	127	30
Jin Jeong*	291.6	71	38	74	54	45	125	16
Miguel Angel Jimenez	301.0	54	41	66	53	53	124	10
Dustin Johnson	327.5	2	49	24	55	39	125	16
Richard S Johnson	285.3	75	53	2	53	53	130	56
Zach Johnson	291.3	72	50	14	50	72	127	30
Robert Karlsson	317.8	11	38	74	59	13	130	56
Martin Kaymer	303.8	48	46	46	59	13	125	16
Simon Khan	306.4	39	48	29	54	45	129	47
Kyung-tae Kim	297.1	64	47	38	58	18	131	59
Soren Kjeldsen	304.3	46	50	14	56	32	128	39
Matt Kuchar	302.6	52	45	55	53	53	124	10
Tom Lehman	303.3	50	51	7	55	39	125	16
Marc Leishman	311.6	22	49	24	58	18	133	69
Shane Lowry	312.0	21	47	38	53	53	126	26
Hunter Mahan	311.5	24	48	29	58	18	134	73
Steve Marino	307.1	37	45	55	54	45	129	47
Graeme McDowell	309.4	27	46	46	61	2	132	66
Rory McIlroy	317.1	12	48	29	61	2	130	56
Phil Mickelson	303.8	48	43	60	49	73	126	26
Hirofumi Miyase	300.3	57	47	38	51	70	125	16
Edoardo Molinari	299.8	59	50	14	62	1	133	69
Colin Montgomerie	287.6	74	47	38	55	39	131	59
Colm Moriarty	304.0	47	41	66	56	32	127	30
Kevin Na	307.5	36	50	14	54	45	127	30
Sean O'Hair	304.9	43	49	24	57	25	121	3
Louis Oosthuizen	319.4	4	55	1	60	8	121	3
Jeff Overton	318.5	6	40	70	57	25	128	39
Tom Pernice Jr	283.6	76	50	14	58	18	131	59
Ian Poulter	295.0	67	46	46	58	18	131	59
Alvaro Quiros	331.0	1	39	71	60	8	132	66
Robert Rock	304.5	44	47	38	57	25	122	7
Charl Schwartzel	311.6	23	46	46	56	32	124	10
Zane Scotland	308.6	30	46	46	49	73	126	26
Adam Scott	311.1	25	51	7	52	65	127	30
John Senden	295.6	66	53	2	61	2	131	59
Peter Senior	292.4	70	48	29	60	8	136	76
Marcel Siem	297.8	63	51	7	53	53	125	16
Vijay Singh	313.0	19	46	46	57	25	129	47
Heath Slocum	299.9	58	45	55	53	53	129	47
Henrik Stenson	296.6	65	52	6	54	45	121	3
Steve Stricker	292.6	69	50	14	49	73	121	3
Toru Taniguchi	294.4	68	43	60	53	53	125	16
Steven Tiley	305.0	42	50	14	53	53	131	59
Bo Van Pelt	312.4	20	48	29	59	13	134	73
Scott Verplank	307.9	33	36	76	52	65	129	47
Camilo Villegas	318.3	9	44	59	56	31	130	66
Nick Watney	308.7	29	53	2	58	18	127	30
Lee Westwood	313.5	18	50	14	54	45	122	7
Tiger Woods	318.1	10	47	37	53	52	126	38
YE Yang	309.1	28	41	66	56	32	129	47

NON QUALIFIERS AFTER 36 HOLES

	Driving Distance	Rank	Fairways Hit	Rank	Greens In Regulation	Rank	Putts	Rank
Jamie Abbott*	284.0	141	25	36	23	134	64	52
Byeong-Hun An*	311.5	35	21	115	25	101	66	92
Phillip Archer	310.8	39	20	127	27	61	67	104
Kurt Barnes	317.0	20	19	142	24	123	68	117
Thomas Bjorn	286.3	136	22	100	27	61	66	92
Jason Bohn	283.0	142	26	21	26	86	66	92
Angel Cabrera	309.8	43	20	127	23	134	63	36
Laurie Canter*	309.5	44	24	60	19	152	68	117
KJ Choi	311.8	32	20	127	24	123	68	117
Eric Chun*	288.5	127	25	36	23	134	62	20
Gary Clark	285.3	137	22	100	24	123	70	142
Tim Clark	284.8	138	21	115	25	101	66	92
Ben Crane	289.5	120	26	21	24	123	61	12
Josh Cunliffe	268.5	155	25	36	19	152	63	36
Ben Curtis	294.8	101	24	60	30	16	70	142
Rhys Davies	296.3	97	25	36	26	86	64	52
Glen Day	276.3	149	24	60	24	123	72	151
Victor Dubuisson*	307.8	47	17	153	27	61	70	142
Jason Dufner	292.8	108	21	115	26	86	69	134
David Duval	303.0	74	20	127	24	123	66	92
Simon Edwards	259.3	156	19	142	19	152	73	154
Ernie Els	301.5	81	27	9	27	61	68	117
Sir Nick Faldo	281.7	143	25	36	25	101	70	142
Gonzalo Fdez-Castano	300.7	84	22	100	23	134	62	20
Darren Fichardt	304.5	63	25	36	24	123	67	104
Hiroyuki Fujita	294.3	103	16	154	22	142	62	20
Jim Furyk	298.3	89	19	142	19	152	60	8
Brian Gay	291.0	115	19	142	24	123	69	134
Mathew Goggin	303.0	74	24	60	25	101	69	134
Tano Goya	287.3	132	25	36	25	101	64	52
Paul Goydos	274.3	150	27	9	26	86	67	104
Bill Haas	289.3	122	26	21	27	61	70	142
Mark F Haastrup	291.5	112	24	60	20	151	62	20
Todd Hamilton	289.5	120	24	60	26	86	67	104
Anders Hansen	284.8	138	21	115	25	101	64	52
Soren Hansen	308.5	45	29	2	29	27	72	151
Padraig Harrington	294.8	101	23	77	25	101	66	92
Tyrrell Hatton*	289.0	125	20	127	19	152	63	36
Gregory Havret	288.3	129	25	36	24	123	65	74
Jean Hugo	271.5	153	23	77	22	142	65	74
Yuta Ikeda	307.0	51	23	77	25	101	69	134
Thongchai Jaidee	291.3	113	23	77	25	101	68	117
Jerry Kelly	292.8	108	23	77	26	86	71	149
Martin Laird	303.3	72	23	77	25	101	72	151
Jose Manuel Lara	306.3	53	20	127	22	142	67	104
Paul Lawrie	295.5	99	21	115	25	101	64	52
Justin Leonard	297.0	91	25	36	27	61	67	104
Thomas Levet	296.5	95	24	60	25	101	69	134
Davis Love III	302.8	78	22	100	28	43	69	134
Sandy Lyle	321.3	8	20	127	29	27	70	142
Gareth Maybin	284.5	140	26	21	25	101	64	52
Ross McGowan	305.3	58	24	60	28	43	68	117
George McNeill	303.8	69	19	142	23	134	68	117
Katsumasa Miyamoto	317.5	15	21	115	26	86	68	117
Francesco Molinari	304.3	64	27	9	28	43	69	134
Ryan Moore	302.7	79	25	36	25	101	68	117
Seung-Yul Noh	316.0	23	21	115	23	134	65	74
Alexander Noren	290.3	118	21	115	22	142	68	117
Koumei Oda	318.3	14	21	115	24	123	62	20
Ryuichi Oda	313.5	28	23	77	27	61	64	52
Geoff Ogilvy	301.5	81	23	77	26	86	65	74
Mark O'Meara	277.3	146	26	21	27	61	65	74
Jae-Bum Park	288.8	126	24	60	22	142	68	117
Cameron Percy	290.3	118	18	151	22	142	66	92
Kenny Perry	310.0	42	20	127	25	101	68	117
Tim Petrovic	270.0	154	22	100	22	142	65	74
DA Points	297.0	91	23	77	29	27	70	142
Ewan Porter	304.3	64	19	142	25	101	74	156
Loren Roberts	273.0	151	24	60	27	61	68	117
Justin Rose	301.5	81	22	100	26	86	64	52
Michael Sim	291.3	113	28	4	27	61	67	104
Shunsuke Sonoda	305.8	54	21	115	29	27	73	154
Paul Streeter	293.3	107	20	127	21	149	63	36
Bubba Watson	318.5	12	20	127	28	43	67	104
Tom Watson	277.0	147	24	60	24	123	65	74
Mike Weir	307.8	47	19	142	26	86	66	92
Tom Whitehouse	296.8	94	24	60	25	101	63	36
Oliver Wilson	295.7	98	19	142	27	61	65	74
Chris Wood	293.8	105	23	77	21	149	62	20

THE OLD COURSE
ST ANDREWS